**WARNING! THE CONTENT OF THIS BOOK CAN CAUSE OUTBURST OF UNCONTROLLABLE LAUGHTER
(CONTAINS GRAPHIC ADULT LANGUAGE)**

Generation X:
URBAN REALITY
Teen Exploits & Comedic Situations

K.D. WILLIAMS

Gotham Books

30 N Gould St.
Ste. 20820, Sheridan, WY 82801
https://gothambooksinc.com/

Phone: 1 (307) 464-7800

© 2023 *K.D Williams*. All rights reserved.

No part of this book may be reproduced, stored in a retrieval system, or transmitted by any means without the written permission of the author.

Published by Gotham Books (November 28, 2023)

ISBN: 979-8-88775-646-2 (P)
ISBN: 979-8-88775-647-9 (E)

Because of the dynamic nature of the Internet, any web addresses or links contained in this book may have changed since publication and may no longer be valid.

The views expressed in this work are solely those of the author and do not necessarily reflect the views of the publisher, and the publisher hereby disclaims any responsibility for them.

This book was inspired by the Legrand Family of Cincinnati, Ohio. Its purpose is to entertain readers with a series of progressive stories about the life and times of a group of incredulous cousins. It's a work of creative, humorous fiction. Furthermore, it goes full circle towards its goal of showing how the genuine aspects of having faith, strong morals, and family values can be a positive influence on a teenager's life.

TABLE OF CONTENT

ABOUT THE BOOK vii

CHAPTER ONE
    THE 911 CALL 1

CHAPTER TWO
    THE "JIG IS UP" 9
    A PREPONDERANCE OF EVIDENCE 10

CHAPTER THREE
    THE COLD-CASE REVENGE A MYSTERY RESOLVED 15

CHAPTER FOUR
    THE DEPARTURE 22
    RODE TRIPPIN 24

CHAPTER FIVE
    A TASTE OF HOLINESS 32

CHAPTER SIX
    HOLY HYPNOSIS 44

CHAPTER SEVEN
    HOME COMING/AUNT ELLA'S HOUSE 49
    THE NEXT MORNING 51

CHAPTER EIGHT
    THE OATMEAL WAR 53
    THE DOG THAT COULD WALK ON WATER 53

CHAPTER NINE
    THE HOG CALLING 57

CHAPTER TEN
    THE COWMAN COM-ETH 66

CHAPTER ELEVEN
    FUNK HITS THE FAN/ SEXUAL HEALING 71

CHAPTER TWELVE
    THE STAR-SPANGLED EXPLOSION 75
    THE DRAMA BEGINS 76

CHAPTER THIRTEEN
    THE DRIVE-BY DROP-OFF 81
    THE GREAT ESCAPE 84

CHAPTER FOURTEEN
    HOT CONFLICTS 87
    SAMANTHA'S SURPRISE 91

CHAPTER FIFTEEN
    THE AVENGERS 93

CHAPTER SIXTEEN
    OPERATION DOOR JAM 97

CHAPTER SEVENTEEN
    HIP-HOP FEVER 100

CHAPTER EIGHTEEN
    LAVADA'S LAMENTATION 104

CHAPTER NINETEEN
    THE ROPE A DOPE 107

CHAPTER TWENTY
    THE FREE-STYLE FREE FALL 112

CHAPTER TWENTY-ONE
    AUNT ELLA'S MESSAGE/ THE CONCLUSION 125
    LESSONS FROM THE BIBLE 126
    THE CONCLUSION 129
    THREE YEARS LATER 131

AUTHOR BIO 134

ABOUT THE BOOK

This book is based on factual events that the author has experienced and his knowledge of African American culture.

A God-Fearing, Cantankerous, elderly woman is asked to undergo a traditional, daunting summer task. Her responsibilities include the 'watchdog effort,' and the use of whatever means necessary to discipline and teach her grandchildren, great-nieces, and great-nephews how to live a Christian way of life.

Their ages range from 10—18, and the desire, reluctance, and necessity for them to remain in her house depends on one major stipulation; they all must attend church services with her every Sunday.

This novel is a collection of diverse, raw, entertaining, humorous stories about family fun, adventure, and the experiences that take place in an urban community in Cincinnati, Ohio.

One of the natural outcomes in life is that every generation of adolescents encounters their share of trials, tribulations, and temptations while growing up. In many cases they are unavoidable, sometimes unpredictable, and sometimes unbelievable. The essence of this book touches on every facet of these experiences.

CHAPTER ONE

THE 911 CALL

When a group of complex personalities are mandated under the same roof for an extended period of time, situations in everyday life can change drastically, and as a result, strange, outlandish behavioral conditioning can lead to situations of mischief, mayhem, and chaos; character differences can range from the wild and reckless to the ridiculous.

During the early 1990's, the recession caused an economic decline that in turn created a drastic change in workforce stability. It challenged the lives and day-to-day living of people across the country.

Moreover, there were two girls whose mother was thinking the worse, but fortunately she had a bit of good luck during these hard times. Her job wasn't shutting down or relocating to Mexico or somewhere overseas; instead, it was just moving to a more established industrial city about sixty miles away from their original home.

When Tamara and Earlene heard the good news, it was a small comfort for them. But they were still considering the fact that they still had to move in with their grandmother across town and endure the antics of their irritating, pain-in-the-ass cousin, Alvin Junior—AKA A. J., who had moved there with his dad and his sister, Danielle just a few months ago. Therefore, their main concern was having to put up with A. J's foolish behavior, and for obvious reasons, they couldn't dismiss their feeling of dread from being around him.

It was the first day of summer and Earlene was already sick of A.J. He was a pest and a clown, and he thought he was a comedian. The jokes he told were dumb, but he still thought he was the hottest sensation since Eddie Murphy. To his friends he was a laugh a minute and fun to be around—whatever he said or did to get a laugh seemed to amuse them. But when it came to Earlene and Tamara, he fell short; he was about as funny as a train wreck.

However, behind his acts of playfulness and joke telling he had a ton of love for his cousins. But all he ever managed to do was get on their last nerve. And as such, he kept pushing Earlene's stress button to the point of being an ongoing ritual.

The event that brought sparks to Earlene's growing disdain for A.J. happened on a Saturday morning in June. The bicycle wreck that occurred that morning could be described better by saying it was a as a tragedy.

Earlene's knowledge of the incident came from an anonymous phone call. Someone saw exactly what happened and told her the bad news. And it was obvious to see, from look of her facial expression that hearing the news made her blood boil. But, when she found out that A.J. wrecked her bike, an immediate urge to kick his ass kicked in.

The story was that Mr. No-hands, No-feet—No-two front teeth, took her bicycle out for a spin through the neighborhood without her permission. The ridiculous part about it was that common sense didn't tell the genius that riding that bike 50mph down a steep hill, and trying to make a 45 degree turn around a corner without using the breaks would wind up with him hitting the ground.

> And that's just how it happened; A.J. hit the ground and rolled like a log off the back of a lumber truck--right into a fire hydrant on the corner. And while he was rolling, Earlene's bike had slid underneath the rolling wheels of a garbage truck. After the bike was pulled from underneath the truck, it was shaped like a pretzel and it could have been submitted as an entry to a museum of abstract art. Even more heart-wrenching was when old, funky Herald the trash man picked it up without thinking twice about how it got there and threw it in the back of the truck with the rest of the trash.

Meanwhile, after the strenuous contemplation of a lie to tell Earlene, A.J. went home and tried to sneak through the back door. He had a blood-soaked paper towel covering his mouth and his two front teeth were missing. He even had scrapes and scares on the side of his face and arms, but before he could say a word to Earlene, she saw the creep, and she didn't waste any time having sympathy for him. As far as she was concerned, what he did was wrong, and he was going to pay!

So, faster than a flash of lightning, she jumped on his ass like a thunderstorm. She grabbed him by his throat and tried to choke the life out of him; his eyes were popping out of his head, and blood was trickling out the side of his mouth. But fortunately, and right in the middle of drawing back her fist to cold-cock him into the middle of next summer, her Grandma came out of her bedroom room and snatched her arm. She grabbed her by the collar, and sat her down in a chair. But, by the time she turned around, A.J. was gone; he disappeared faster than a fugitive on a chain gang.

It was a close call for A.J. this time; that girl was going to tear him a new asshole. But, his dad, Alvin senior, and Grandma Ella did their best to calm Earlene down; and fortunately, they didn't have to use the straitjacket that her Grandma kept in the hall closet. They both knew that Earlene had a temper just like her mother, Erma Jean. Pushing the wrong button on either one of them was like pushing the button on a time bomb for terror.

Even his sister, Danielle tried to show her concern for Earlene. She wanted to show her that her heart was in the right place and save her weasel of a brother's life. So, she made a cold pitcher of cherry Kool-Aid and brought her a glass to cool her off. But in all practicality, she was more than likely thinking that it would quench her thirst for the taste of blood.

Her Uncle Alvin reassured her that he would buy her a new bicycle and punish A.J. when he caught up with him. And her Grandma promised to have a long talk with A.J. about her bike, as well as the many other things he did to aggravate her.

Anyway, Earlene knew that their intentions were good and that they meant well, but she also knew A.J., and she knew that getting through to him was like peeling back the layers of a rotten onion. To put it plain and simple, the idea of revenge was still firmly planted in the back of her mind, and she just knew that whenever she caught up with the rat again—he was going to be an astronaut, and she had the rocket-ship to fly his ass to the moon.

Three days later, A.J. surfaced. Everyone knew he was hiding somewhere in the attic, but as long as he stayed out of their sight, he couldn't cause any more trouble. Furthermore, the anger and resentment that Earlene had been feeling subsided to a smaller degree, which is just what A.J. hoped would happen. But he was still acting like a callus, cold-hearted creep when he saw Earlene again, and he pretended to have no recollection of what happened three days ago. Thus, there was no apology from him, nor a gram of what could be considered remorse.

So, after two or three days of watching that "Weasel" lollipop around the house like he didn't have a care in the world, something in Earlene's mind clicked. It told her that: "that fool didn't even get a punishment--he got a reprieve from an injustice." "Uh, Hun," she said to herself, I knew this was going to happen. And from that moment on, she knew that sooner or later she would have to deliberate her style of justice.

The two of them were frequently running into each other all through the day. Every time they met; AJ approached her with a different corny joke--trying to break the ice between them. And in every instance, Earlene told him that she didn't want to hear his stupid joke. But even more perplexing to her was the fact that she really didn't have a chance to stomp a mud-hole in his ass on those particular occasions, because, as it turned out, Grandma was always somewhere nearby with open ears.

Anyway, A.J. couldn't stop being a pest. He was like a junkie with an addiction. Something told him to keep on messing with that girl. One reason why he did it is because of the rejection she dismissed him with; it upset him to the point where--if he couldn't make her laugh-- he was going to make her life miserable. And sure enough, A.J. took it to the next level. He came up with plan to piss her off.

He knew that every morning at five o'clock she would go to the bathroom. Her routine was like clockwork, it never failed. The loud squeaking noises on the floor coming from the wooden boards upstairs would wake him every time she walked to the bathroom. This time, he thought, I'm going to make that noise stop. It's going to sound a little different this time. Instead of hearing that squeaking, the floor was going to go Snap, Crackle, and Pop!

So, later on, on that long, hot tumultuous night, A.J. went through with his plan to fortify his comedic skill, and to show her that he was the 'King of The House,' but he had no way of knowing that he was opening up an invitation to an ass whooping. Anyway, this dastardly dude turned his video console up on full blast to drown out the sound of a short-handled rip-saw that he used to cut the floorboard on the second-floor ceiling. He cut half-way through four wide slats of old, rotten wood of the floorboard next to the upstairs bathroom. After that he went upstairs and placed a fury throw rug over the area that he cut.

Then, he went to bed, and it was up to Earlene to literally fall into his trap. Six hours later, and as usual, Earlene got up and headed toward the bathroom. And as usual, the squeaking from the floor was back. She walked down to the front of the bathroom door and stepped on the throw rug and it felt good to her bare feet. But, as she stood there for a moment, something seemed strange to her. She looked down and saw the throw beneath her feet and got a funny vibe, because it hadn't been there before. Nevertheless, she noticed that the squeaking had stopped, but in the split-second that followed something gave-away, and all of a sudden, she heard something snap, then she heard the floor crackle, and a micro-second later there was a loud, thunderous POP, echoing through the hall.

Earlene fell halfway through the floor up to her elbows and was screaming at the top of her lungs. She was scared to death. Her legs were kicking, twisting, and dangling from the second-floor ceiling. When A.J. heard the noise, he was laying in his bed laughing at the scene he was visualizing When he finally got up, he approached the disaster area with caution and looked up at the bottom of Earlene's feet. Then he facetiously asked her: "Damn Earlene, what happened! How in the hell did you get stuck in the floor? Well, anyway, I bet you got time to listen to one of my jokes now, don't you? I got a riddle for you. Listen to this one Earlene: What do you call a monkey walking through a minefield?" But all he could hear was the muffled sound of her cursing like a crazed psychopath.

However, eager to tell her the punchline he said: "you call it a Baa-Boom! You get it, a Baa-Boom! Ah ha, ha, ha, ha, ha, ha, ha!" Furthermore, right after he told his corny joke, adding insult to injury, he couldn't resist the temptation to tickle the bottom of Earlene's feet while she was hanging there in limbo. And when he did, she kicked at him and twisted and turned her body from side to side, desperately trying to free herself from that hole in the floor. Her vicious response to him was: "I know you had something to do with this, A.J., and when I catch you, it's All Over For Your ASS"!

So, around about 5:30 that morning, Earlene broke free from her state of temporary incarceration. She held both of her arms straight up over her head and shoulders and kicked her legs. It was painful, but it worked—she slid through and landed on the floor below. By this time, A.J. was nowhere to be found.

Earlene was enraged. When she got to her feet, she swore that this time, nobody was going to stop her from giving that bicycle stealing, smart-ass little runt the beat-down he deserved.

She was ready for action, she had a plan, and she knew just how to catch that RAT! In short, she enticed him with just the right bait to make him come to her.

She had a grim look on her-face and her main motivation was the picture that lingered in her mind of a tombstone in a graveyard with A.J.'s name written on it. To sum it up, at this point in time, she didn't mind doing hard-time for murder.

Well, it took a while, but Earlene didn't have to wait long at all for that boy to show up. It took her about ten minutes to bait a trap that she knew he was bound to fall in to. She set her trap in the living room by setting out the pitcher of Kool-Aid that Danielle made the night before, and some paper cups that her Grandma used to make ice-balls.

Then she set it on the cocktail table in the front room and turned the TV on. Next, she got one of her Michael Jackson D V D's, put it in the player and turned up the volume. Then she turned off the lights using the wall switch next to the sofa. Finally, she climbed to the top of the back end of the sofa and stood there in the darkness with a frying pan in her hand and waited for AJ to hear the music and come through the doorway.

Well, as it turned out, it happened just like she expected. It didn't take long for A.J. to hear the music and come running to the living room. He looked inside and saw the pitcher of Kool-Aid sitting on the table and hesitated for a moment because it was dark inside. But, he didn't see Earlene anywhere around and he couldn't resist the sound of the music, plus he was thirsty. So, at his own risk, he cautiously stuck his head inside and did a quick scan of the furniture to see if anyone was in there. But how he missed seeing those two, big bare feet of Earlene's on top of the couch at the end of the room was a marvel in itself.

So, beyond his better judgment, A.J. got Jiggy with it. He started dancing and prancing; finger popping and booty bopping; unaware of Earlene's stalking presence, high above and behind him. Well, soon afterwards the music sounded so good to him that he forgot all about Earlene chasing him, and he decided that it was refreshment time, and, that's right— 'He drank the Kool-Aid'. After that, he went right back into his Michael Jackson imitation and he moon-walked all the way back into the arms of his beholder. Suddenly the lights came on, but damned if he saw her coming.

Earlene jumped on that boy's back like she was a cowboy riding a bucking Bronco. She started banging him upside his head with that frying pan, and he fell to the floor with her still on his back. She screamed and shouted at him: "I Got Your Ass Now, Don't I, You Little Creep!" Then she stood up and jumped on that boy's back like it was a trampoline. To top it off, she kicked him in the two major orifices of his body--his big mouth and his little ass.

After that excruciating three-minute bout, an imaginary bell must have rung: Ding, Ding, Ding, because Earlene went to her neutral corner to get her second wind. She had a seat on the couch with AJ still laying on the floor sprawled out on his belly-- petrified and unable to move. He looked like a Pygmy that just got stampeded by a herd of elephants.

The only weapon at his disposal was the telephone lying on the floor in front of him. He laid there knowing that he had to do something quick before the bell rang to start round two. So out of desperation, he grabbed the phone and quickly dialed 911.

However, he wanted to save face, because he knew that Earlene was still in the room listening to him when he picked up the phone, and he didn't want to sound like a punk when he talked to the operator, so he changed the true context of what had happened in the conversation to sound more favorable for him.

Hello, 911 emergency."

"Hello, 911."

"Yes, can I help you?"

"Yeah, Yall Better Come Get Her Before I Kill Her!"

"Sir, what's the problem?" How can I help you?

"There's been an Attempt On My Life!"

"What happened, sir?"

"It's my cousin, Earlene. She Dunn went crazy! She jumped on my back, knocked me down, and started beating me in the head with a frying pan. Then she jumped on my back and kicked me everywhere. I'm gonna Kill her if Yall don't come and get her!"

"Well sir, where is she at right now?"

"She's sitting on the couch sipping on a cup of Kool-Aid.

"Well, sir, where are you at?"

"I'm lying here on the floor with a Knot In My Ass!"

"Sir, are there any weapons in the house?"

"Weapons? No—I don't think so. Oh Yeah! My daddy's "nine" is around here somewhere, and if I find it, she's gonna have more holes in her than a piece of Swiss Cheese!"

Earlene bolstered with contempt when she heard him say that. She shouted: "Shut up and get off the phone, you little Weasel!" And A.J. was so emotionally charged that his only recourse was:

"Ooow! I'm gonna get you Earlene; I swear I'm gonna get you!"

Awakened by the distraction coming from the front room was Grandma. She came from her bedroom in the back, and when she saw all the destruction around her, and the casualty of war at her feet, she snatched the phone from A.J. Then she started in on both of them. Boy get your devilish behind off the floor. Earlene, what are you doing down here? Yall better clean up this mess and be ready for church in the morning!

Lord have mercy, Yall are gonna to send me to my grave!" Then she put the phone to her ear to see who was on the other end. "Hello, who is this?" The voice answered: "This is the 911 operator, ma'am. Is everything alright?" "No honey, but it will be, even if I have to find a switch and beat the meat off somebody's behind in here! There's no need for the police; I've got this honey." "Well if you need us, give us a call." "Thank you, honey, goodbye."

Ms. Ella had a troubled mind after that, but she still went out of her way to clean up the mess in the living room. And while she was doing that, she looked up at the ceiling and started mumbling these words: "Lord Jesus, I keep telling that boy to leave that girl and her things alone—he just won't listen; he's just too hard headed! I don't know why he keeps on doing the things he does Lord.

And Lord, I knew deep in my heart that it was just a matter of time before that girl KICKED THAT LITTLE BOY'S ASS!"

CHAPTER TWO
THE "JIG IS UP"

While the flames of fury were boiling down to a simmer on the West side of town, two more feisty fireballs were waiting to be picked up on the East side of town. The history of sibling rivalry between this brother and sister tandem during the past few months had been, to say the least "Unbelievable."

These two kids lived with their Grandmother as well. Six months ago they came to live with her, and as time went by, there was no mention about the return of their parents. And as such, they soon turned into two nerve-racking, problematic kids; one day after another was been more unbelievable than the next. But, she was finally getting a break; this morning she got them ready for an extended leave of absence. And within the next two hours, David and Samantha were on their way to church with a group of their cousins.

In retrospect, to summarize the natural order of events that led up them being on that bus ride to church came about partly because of the destruction of Samantha's birthday party. It started several months ago due to the treachery that Samantha allegedly imposed on her brother. She had been accused of using up all but a drop of Maple syrup for him to put on his pancakes. That's what sparked the rivalry that escalated into an all- out -war, and a plot by Samantha to literally transform her brother into a snowman in the backyard.

And as such, it wasn't until after his transformation back into a normal human being that his loss of memory was restored. After that came a discovery of facts that led to the proof he needed to re-open the files on a Cold-Case. And as soon as that was established, his revenge was right at the forefront when the time came to ruin her birthday party.

A PREPONDERANCE OF EVIDENCE

David's reappearance had been just as mysterious as his disappearance. Sam and her Grandma had just come through the front door when they heard a loud shriek of terror coming from the backyard. A large groundhog burrowing underground and around David's feet had awakened him from his deep sleep. But what really made him hysterical was seeing a huge black bird from the corner of his eye—it was perched on his shoulder—pecking away at a stale pancake that was slipping from underneath a pair of shaded sunglasses covering his eyes.

He had to have set a new Olympic record for the 100- meter dash when he made eye to eye contact with that bird, because he busted out of that suit of snow running like a quarter horse out of the starting gate. Furthermore, if his Grandmother hadn't been there to open the back door at the exact same time he was headed towards it, there would have been a new opening right through the middle.

Grandma was shocked when she realized that it was David that shot by her at the speed of light. "Holy Jesus and Mary" she shouted. "What in the Devil is going on?" So, she followed him through the house (with Samantha close behind). He was shedding his frozen clothes all over the house-- in front of the fireplace in the living room, in the hallway, and finally, next to the heat vent on the floor of his bedroom-- where he stood with a blanket wrapped around him.

He was shivering from head to toe. His teeth were chattering and he was mumbling incoherent words-- making no sense whatsoever. Nevertheless, his Grandma tried to interrogate him about his whereabouts for the past week. And sure enough, her interrogation was complemented with a strong- Oscar- winning backup performance by Samantha.

Grandma was in disbelief-- she couldn't make heads or tells out of what he was saying. But, she also noticed that whenever he heard Sam's voice in the background, he became enraged, and he kept shouting and repeating the same thing: Sa Sa,Sa—am- k-k-k-kno--kno-s-s! kk kk—ill H h-h h—er. I—I--I I- —Ha-ha-ha h h-ATE—He-he h-h—er!

But, his Grandma just walked away with a puzzled look on her face. The only thing she could do is what she knew how to do best—nurse him back into good health. She fixed him a can of soup, fed it to him, and put him to bed with a lot of warm blankets covering him.

Well, so far Sam's plot to keep her Grandma from knowing that she knew where David was all along was working. "Agent 007" was always somewhere nearby tuned into every word that was being said between the two of them. But she knew she had to come up with a new strategy soon to keep her Grandma from finding out what happened to David for all of that time.

And as such, the clever junior CIA operative set the wheels in her head in motion. Then she finally devised a plan to cover her behind, and that was to be extra nice to David tomorrow morning, and to convince him that he had been real sick. Her goal was to make him believe that whatever he thought had happened to him was just a bad dream.

Well, that same night, the 'Human Popsicle' tossed and turned in his sleep. He would moan and groan in anguish, and there was an occasional outburst of fanatical screams and yelling from time to time, but his Grandma was soon by his side to calm him down.

The next morning David woke up to warm rays of sunshine glimmering on his face. He yawned and stretched his arms and legs and sat up in bed. Then he inhaled a deep breath of air and let it out. That's when he picked up on the smell of pancakes cooking in the kitchen. Ah yes, he thought, he was back in his natural domain, and his thoughts and the feeling in his legs were coming back to normal.

A few minutes later, there was a knock at his door. Samantha busted in and was smiling like 'Little Miss Sunshine.' She was carrying a plate of pancakes; soaked with butter and covered with maple syrup. "Hello, my dear brother, "she said cheerfully. David was stunned. He couldn't believe his eyes or ears; he was flabbergasted, and his mouth opened up wider than the Lincoln Tunnel from shock. And naturally, the enticing smell of those pancakes added to the lingering affect that had his bottom lip drooping down to his chin.

Anyway, in the back of his mind he was still thinking that (after all she did to me, this rotten heifer has the nerve to act like everything is alright. On top of that, she's got the gall to be so lively and carefree about it.)

He scornfully said, "I didn't say you could come in here." But Samantha ignored the tone of voice and skillfully went to work warming up the cold blood running through his veins, and she put on a command performance while it.

"Have you been having those bad dreams again, David?"

"What! What are you talking about?"

"Grandma says you've been real, real, sick."

"Huh! —I've been what!"

"Oh yeah, David. You had a fever and you've been tossing and turning and hollering in your sleep for over a week now."

"But the last thing I remember is building a snowman in the backyard."

"Yep, and that's when you got sick."

"But something else happened that I can't remember."

"Well, here go your pancakes, David. Grandma made-um especially for you, cause you been sick. I mean really, really, really, really sick!"

He was totally confused now. The bomb that Samantha just dropped on him blew his mind, and he didn't know whether to swallow the deceitful pill she had administered or that delicious stack of pancakes in front of him. But those choices didn't last long, because after thinking about it for a moment or two, he gave in; he couldn't wait to start swallowing that stack of pancakes. So, he filled his belly and nodded off into a comma-like sleep.

The plan that Sam devised worked like a charm. When Grandma entered the room to talk to him, she was too late. She still wanted to find out where he had been for all this time, but he was fast asleep. It was all over for that notion. So, she just pulled the cover over the 'boy wonder,' kissed him on the forehead, and took his dirty dishes to the kitchen.

The days that followed turned into weeks. Samantha stuck to her academy performance and no one was the wiser. After a while, both David and Grandma had forgotten about what was so important for them to know.

When March 1st rolled around, all the snow had melted and Samantha was preparing for her birthday party. And with all the snow gone, there wasn't much for the snowman architect to do.

Today was Samantha's birthday. She was anxiously waiting for her Grandmother to come back from the store with party favors and decorations for her birthday party. But David was still wandering aimlessly around the house from one window to another--looking outside for enough snow to make a snowball.

This boy had it bad; he had a "Snowman Jones" and watching him go "Cold Turkey" was an awful sight to see.

Anyway, Grandma finally made it home. She came through the door with a bag full of party trimmings and food for the party. They asked David to help with the decorations, but he was too stubborn to help and he continued to mope around the house in a deep funk--looking out one window and then another, in search of a glimmer of the long-gone snow.

However, in due time, and like a sign from up above, he noticed something from the back window. There was a flickering of light coming from a dark object sticking out from the ground. It was right in front of the oak tree in the middle of the backyard, and it brought David's curiosity to a peak. Therefore, he couldn't resist going outside to see what it was.

Low and behold, there they were, his missing pair of sunglasses. They were reflecting the sunlight. But, how did they get out here he thought, and as he got closer, he bent down to pick them up and noticed two foot-prints embedded in the ground in front of the oak tree. Then he saw that they were the same size as his. So, for the sake of curiosity, he put his feet in the prints to see if they were a match. And Bam! They fit so well that it jogged his memory like a bolt of lightning, thus, his moment of truth had arrived!

"Real, real sick"! Yeah Right," is what he murmured to himself in a sarcastic tone. Then he re-played his memory back to what had happened to him on that day. He remembered building a snowman in the backyard. He remembered that the weather suddenly changed. He remembered running to the back door to get out of the cold, and he remembered being soaked with the water in the bucket that fell on his head. But he couldn't remember seeing the baseball bat that swung down from the garage ceiling to rattle his brain, and to the point where he could remember what he just now remembered. But he had a very good idea now. He summed it up with one word—Samantha!

He was naturally consumed with an overwhelming desire for revenge. Some-how, some way he knew he had to get even. Thus, his attitude suddenly changed from being a mild-mannered detective to being a devious, underhanded creep. His new discovery of evidence demanded immediate satisfaction, and guess who was number one on the receiving end of his list—his rotten, calculating little sister.

Nevertheless, the 'ice man' played it cool. He went back in the house with a new attitude; cool, calm, and collected and he resumed playing the natural, block-head brother role.

When he went back in the house, his behavior towards his Grandma and Samantha changed from stubborn and selfish to helpful and cooperative. He offered to help with the party decorations, and that drew suspicion in Samantha's mind. They couldn't figure him out, and Samantha couldn't stop looking at him with an eyebrow raised and wondering what he was really up to.

Furthermore, David didn't know exactly how he was going to do it, but the destruction of this birthday party was his major objective. He would have to improvise a plan as he went along, but he was determined to do any and everything possible to get revenge.

CHAPTER THREE

THE COLD-CASE REVENGE
A MYSTERY RESOLVED

Well, it didn't take a long for Samantha and her Grandma to put their trust in David. After they got over their suspicious thoughts about him wanting to help, they allowed him to hang up decorations and set out party hats, whistles, and blow-up balloons. Other than that, Grandma needed him to get the sheet-cake on the back seat of her car.

When David saw the sheet cake on the back seat he slid it towards him, and when he did, he saw a brown paper bag with a bottle of medicine sticking out. It had turned over and was beginning to spill out. He wasn't sure what it was until he pulled it out the bag. So, when he looked at the bottle, it had Milk of Magnesia written on it; whenever he saw his Grandma drink this stuff, he knew that soon afterwards she'd be running to the bathroom.

He paused for a moment and thought to himself- 'Hum—This is just the stroke of luck I need. And from that moment on, the wheels in his head were spinning, and out popped those devilish horns of his. So, when he added two and two together- somehow it added up three, and in the next few minutes, he was carrying a white sheet cake with white icing in the house, but it was covered with that white, chalky colored Milk of Magnesia.

Everything was coming together as planned in the house. Samantha was nearly done with her decorations, and Grandma had a pot of hot-dogs simmering on the stove. As for "King Rat," David, he had spread that bottle on Milk of Magnesia on top of that cake so evenly that no one could tell the difference. He was going to make sure that all of Samantha's greedy, creepy, friends got a good dose of this medicine.

Well, he sat the cake on the dining room table and slowly stepped back. Then he turned around and looked at Samantha with a conniving grin on his face, then he walked away acting cool as a cucumber-- Samantha just stared at him with her eyebrow raised wondering what he was up to.

But regardless of her curiosity, Samantha realized that the party time was approaching, so she hopped to feet and ran to her bedroom to change clothes. And right after that, sooner than she expected, the doorbell rang—some of her friends had arrived early.

Surprisingly, David was there to greet them at the door, and as such, he was being the typical nuisance that he always was around her friends. He opened the door and looked down his nose at them like they were a group of subhuman species-- he cut and rolled his eyes at each member of the rat pack as they were coming through the door.

The first of her friends to be scoured by his contempt was Fat Elmo. He was five-foot tall and four-feet-wide and eleven-year-old. He grunted and snorted like a pig when he ate and David couldn't stand him. The next goofball through the door was Weird Wayne. He was six-feet tall, eleven years old, and he looked like a long strip of bacon. Not to mention that everything he wore smelled like piss.

Next, there was that butt digging, four-eyed Fred. He was an average size kid to be eleven, but he was as blind as a bat; he wore glasses with an extra thick lens in them but he knocked over everything that wasn't nailed down. Heading up the rear of the pack was Silly Sarah; she laughed at everything that amused her and everything that didn't amuse anybody else. Then there was Buffy, A.K.A (Scruffy Buffy) who dressed like an old bag-lady-- she looked like a Raggedy-Ann doll, and her favorite past-time was picking buggers and eating them when she didn't think anybody was watching. And finally, there was that big mouth, nerve-racking Talk-a-Lot Tonya. She was the Queen of gossip, and she could talk faster than the speed of sound.

Anyway, just as the front door shut, Samantha's bedroom door opened. She made her grand entrance wearing her new birthday dress and new shoes, and in a matter of seconds, the whole house was filled with laughter from the sound of exuberant children. And as such, within a matter of minutes, the talking, laughing, and yelling got louder and louder. It was so loud in the house that David stuck his fingers in his ears to drown out the noise.

And while doing that, he started walking down the hall to his bedroom to observe those soon to be funky kids from the privacy of his bedroom. He couldn't wait for his Grandma to cut that 'damned cake' and for Samantha's greedy friends to start stuffing their faces.

But, while he was waiting for phase 1 to take place, he started on phase 2 of his plan. Moreover, with music playing; whistles blowing; balloons bursting, and the constant, screeching high shrill of laughter going on, it had gotten to be too much for Grandma as well.

She finally calmed them down and got them to shut up, and in the next few minutes, she had them all the sitting at the dining room table in front of the birthday cake. Then she lit the candles on the cake and started them off in a chorus of Happy Birthday.

While all of this was going on, Samantha's, rat of a brother put his plan into action. From the look of his meticulous handy work, you could tell that he was up to no good. He unscrewed the outside faceplate from the bathroom doorknob; he took it apart and detached the locking mechanism from the inside doorknob; then he screwed the faceplate back on.

Finally, he slid the outside doorknob back on the stem. The result was a loosely fitted doorknob hanging on the doorknob stem. Furthermore, with the door locked from the inside, no-one could get in without the key that he had tied to a shoestring hung around his neck.

After everything was set, he went to his bedroom across the hall and all he had to do was sit and wait, and watch to see which one of Samantha's funky friends would be first to run to the bathroom.

Samantha had just blown out the candles on her cake and made her wish. After that, the sound of eight hungry kids, gorging their faces with hot dogs, potato chips, punch, and cake and ice cream was heard for the next thirty minutes—it sounded like feeding time at the zoo.

Likewise, a party of this caliber usually has what's known as a 'Table Pimp' to take charge of the left-over food and such, two of the most scandalous Table Pimps' this side east of the Mississippi River were Fat Elmo and Weird Wayne. They were the self-appointed moochers of this party. They were the youngest and most astute party going rogues in the neighborhood. Before they had even finished eating, they were fussing about the leftover food they were taking home with them.

Meanwhile, they filled their bellies and got ready for the fun that was about to begin. First, they watched Sam open her presents. She got dolls, roller blades, a CD player, some puzzles, and some board games, and she was happy and very pleased them. But, right after that, Grandma brought out a game that they could all play together. It was called "Twister." It was a game that had a large, thick sheet of plastic covered with multi-colored circular dots.

It had a control board with a direction arrow attached that the players had to spin. Whatever color the arrow landed on would be the spot where the player was to place either their hand or foot. The object of the game was for them to all play together without falling.

Grandma got them started with the first spin and showed them how to play it. But soon afterward, and after all the stretching and twisting from one color to another, she realized that she wasn't a getting any younger and retired for the evening. The kids kept on falling on her tired, aching back, and despite them begging her to stay and play some more, Grandma got off the floor, shook her head, and limped away rubbing her hip.

Meanwhile, David was carefully tuned-in to what was going on in the front room. He had just wolfed down three hot dogs and was patiently waiting for the moment when that mild laxative would have its strong effect. Pretty soon it would start churning in the bellies of those creeps, and he wanted to see the expression on their faces when they exploded like a volcano in their draws.

Grandma had just passed by his room headed toward her bedroom, but the party wasn't over yet. The little "hood-rats" were still playing out front, and his party was just about to begin. So, he sat back in his chair, thought of what he'd do when the moment came and grinned like a Rotten Grinch.

Well, the law of physics states that: "for every action, there is an equal and opposite reaction." But the reaction that came from Samantha's funky friends after eating the laxative on top of that birthday cake was stupendous. It was "more powerful than a locomotive," and it had them ready to leap to the bathroom in a single bound. These kids were not going to forget this birthday party any-time soon.

It was Elmo's turn to play and Silly Sarah was spinning the dial. It landed on a red dot, which is where Elmo had to place his foot. The closest red dot to him was between Fred and Tonya, but to get to it meant that he had to bring his right leg over the top of Samantha's head and down to the other side of Wayne and straddle his back.

Well, between the time Elmo got his fat leg up and over the top of Samantha's head was when the first explosion erupted.

That fat little kid let out a loud, long explosion of gas that shook the front room window, rattled the dishes in the China Cabinet, and had a smell that could've gagged a maggot.

And sure enough, Samantha can thank her lucky stars that she wasn't an inch taller because she probably would have wound up deaf or temporarily blind for the next few months. Instead, the fuming hot gas whizzed across the back of her head and caused the short hair at the base of her neck to stand to attention.

"Ooh! You farted on me, Elmo!" she shouted. Elmo was so embarrassed and blushing so much that his facial expression turned from red to deep purple. And naturally, he lied about it. He shouted: "Unt un! That wasn't me; that was Wayne!"

Nevertheless, a few seconds later, the whole intertwined structure had collapsed and everyone hit the floor. They were screaming and shouting at each other with fury. Hysteria broke out, and bodies pummeled, stomachs grumbled, and more and more gas rumbled.

Tempers flared and damned if these kids didn't know how to swear. They were all guilty of making the house smell like a funk-factory, but they had no idea who the culprit was that made them all loose in the caboose.

After a while, it looked like a thick cloud of gas had filled the room. It smelled so bad that the wallpaper was peeling from the kitchen walls, and If there were any flies around, their deaths had to have been quick and painless.

In fact, Samantha thought it wise to open the front door to let some fresh air in, and similarly, David thought it wise to pinch his nose before sticking his head out the door of his room to see what was going on. That's when he saw fat Elmo wobbling down the hall to the bathroom.

He hurried to the bathroom door and turned the knob in desperation to get inside, but to his surprise, the knob came off the stem right into his hand. He looked at the knob in his hand, dropped it, and immediately began banging on the bathroom door and started hollering at the top of his lungs. And during that time, David was standing across the hall, snickering like a circus clown; he took pleasure in watching that boy go through his panic attack.

In the same manner, throughout Elmo's twilight zone experience, he felt the eyes of people looking at him from two directions. He looked down the hall and saw the kids watching in silent disbelief, but even more scary was the feeling he got from the eyes of that fiendish grin of David's.

And just like that, it was time for David's performance. And with no concern about disturbing his Grandma in her bedroom, he started singing like one of the Temptations.

"Shake Your Ass! -- Shake it Fast! -- Shake Your Ass! --Show Me What Cha Working With! --Ah -- Show me What Cha Working With--Shake Your Ass! -- Shake It Fast-- Show Me What Your Working With, I said show me What-cha Working With, Fat Boy!"

Then this nutty kid made a Mojo move. He jumped up and did an about-face maneuver in mid-air, landed on his feet, and shook his butt right in front of that little Boy's face.

Elmo was in shock, and during David's performance he had forgotten all about using the bathroom. But when he finally snapped out of it, he slowly swung his short, stubby arm around to feel his behind and realized that it was too late. Two pounds of shit in his underwear.

Little Elmo stood there looking pitiful, helpless and lost. He was so embarrassed that tears started rolling down his face, and then he wobbled to the front room, grabbed his coat and ran out the door.

Samantha and her friends were standing at the other end of the hallway watching. They were smitten by David's sudden impromptu performance and humiliation tactic. And by now, all of these kids were feeling the full effect of the laxative they unknowingly gobbled down.

To make his point, David showed them the only key to the bathroom on the shoestring tied around his neck. Even more noticeable was the way he kept tossing the bathroom doorknob in the air like a baseball. That sight let them know that it was all over as far as using the bathroom. So, they grabbed their coats and ran out the front door like rats jumping from a sinking ship.

Everyone, but Samantha. She stood her ground right where she was and squared off with David. She was at one end of the hallway, and he was at the other end. It looked like a scene right out of a Western. "The Good, the Bad, and How in Hell do I Get in the Damn Bathroom."

All of a sudden, Samantha shouted: "Give me that doorknob, David!" David Calmly said: "Unt un," and continued tossing the doorknob in the air like a baseball. Samantha shouted again: "Give it to me, Punk!" David smiled graciously, and in another mellow tone he said: "Nope." Then she yelled at the top of her lungs," Grandma!" But Grandma didn't budge.

As far as they knew, she was still in her bedroom sleeping. Then David took the sunglasses from his back pocket and held them out for Samantha to see and he asked her: "Do you know where I found my sunglasses?" Samantha's quick, smart-aleck response was: "Yeah, on a store Dummy, Dummy!" David just smiled, shook his head and said, "Unt un."

And incredibly, the next move Samantha made went by so fast that the only way anyone could have seen it is on an instant replay camera. She streaked down the hall like a flash of light, kicked David in the leg, caught the doorknob in mid-air, and put it on the stem and tried to open the door. But she couldn't open it because it was locked from inside. And now, being angry as ever, she turned around to see David dangling the bathroom key on that shoestring in the air high above her head.

By this time, neither one of them noticed Grandma peeping at them from around the corner, and Samantha leaped and leaped and leaped for that key and couldn't reach it. Then she kicked and kicked and kicked at David's legs to get him to drop the key until, Oops—it happened! Samantha suddenly realized what she had done--she had a big pile of party poop in her panties, and it was running down the back of her leg.

She let out a loud, sorrowful cry, and sobbing like a baby she shouted with tears in her eyes, "Grandma!"

And, once again, David, he couldn't resist rubbing salt in the wound of this humiliating situation. The Rap-star was compelled to do one more performance. So, wasting no time at all, he started singing: Shake Your Ass! -- Shake it Fast! -- Shake Ya Ass! But, unfortunately, that's as far as he got.

All of a sudden, there was a loud noise that sounded like gunfire-- K-POW—Then a painful sounding "AHHH.... SHIT" came out of David's mouth. He looked behind him and saw his Grandma standing there holding a thick, leather razor strap, and then, Grandma shouted: "SHOW ME WHAT YA WORKING WITH!"

And, he showed her just what he was working with and how fast he could run when he streaked straight out the front door. And as he did, Grandma stood at the front door and watched him hide behind cars, trees, houses, and there was even an unsuccessful attempt at trying to hide down a man-hole cover. Nevertheless, to show him that she meant business, she walked down to the end of the driveway, stood there, and shouted: 'Don't let me catch your ass in the street!"

CHAPTER FOUR
THE DEPARTURE

It was time for them to go. Samantha looked at her grandmother with sad eyes and said, "I'm going to miss you Grandma." Then David spoke his heart as well, "I'm going to miss you too Grandma." Then they both put their arms around her and held her tight. Grandma welled up inside and her voice was filled with sadness when she said, "I'm going to miss you babies too."

Then Samantha backed away from her--and sobbing and trembling with fear she said, "I love you Grandma." Grandma said, "I love you too Samantha." Then she ran to her Grandma again, wrapped her arms around her waist and held on to her tight. Grandma held her head to her bosom, stroked her hair and soothed away her fear. "Come on now, she said. We'll be back together soon. The time will just fly by. You and your brother will have so much fun that you won't even miss me, and I'll call you in a few days to see how you're doing, O'K, I promise."

After hearing that, Samantha was relieved. She wiped the tears from her face and gave her grandma a big smile. Then she said, O'K, Grandma, I'll be waiting for you to call. Then Grandma stood at the front door and watched them walk to the bus. As David was getting on bus she noticed he was wearing that same pair of muddy gym-shoes that he came there with, but it was too late to stop him-- he was already on the bus. He slapped Alvin a high-five and immediately ran to the back of the bus to and sat down next to A.J. Then Alvin stepped off the bus and spoke to his Aunt Jan. He said "Hi, Aunt Jan," and she responded "High, Alvin. Hey Alvin, will you make sure that boy puts on his good pair of shoes before he gets to church? "No problem, Auntie, I will." "You all have a good time, and be careful driving, Alvin."

Well, as soon as Samantha got on the bus, she found the nerve to square off with Alvin. She got to the top step, two feet in front of his face and said, "you heard my, Grandma! You better drive this bus like you got some sense, and Don't be Speeding!" But coming from a family with five sisters, Alvin just did what comes naturally. He eased back in his seat, looked her up and down and said: "Go sit your little Peter Pan behind down so I can drive this bus." Then he started the bus, looked straight ahead at the road, and said, (I'm on a mission from God!). Samantha sighed with an exasperating 'Oh Boy.' She rolled her eyes; looked at him like he was a nut; and sauntered down the aisle towards the back of the bus.

Meanwhile, in the very last seats of the bus, David had sat in a seat next to Alvin Junior--aka A.J. Although it was the first time they'd met, they took to each other like fish take to water. So, within minutes of them getting to know each other, A.J. found out that David's middle name was, 'Alafia,' and automatically called him D.A. for short.

Earlene, Tamara, and Danielle were all sitting in the middle seats gabbing on and on about all the things they were going to do this summer. But when Samantha reached their seats, she was acting timid and kind of fearful of them. It was her first time meeting them, and she was youngest member of the bunch; however, they all took the time to welcome her and make her feel at ease.

So, as they were all getting to know her, they eventually got comfortable. But, soon afterwards, they looked toward the front of the bus and saw Alvin pop a James Brown tape in his cassette player and put on his headphones; then came the sunglasses. Those were the signs from a previous experience, and it let them know they were going on one of the wildest bus rides of their lives.

Meanwhile, Grandma Williams was still at the front door with a bewildered look on her face. She was trying to figure out where she saw that raggedy-ass bus before. Then it came to her--it was the same broke down jitney that was parked in the empty lot next to her sister, Ella's house.

She busted out laughing and started talking to herself. (lord, somebody must have been doing a whole lot of praying, she thought, because whatever they did to get that thing up and running was short of a miracle).

RODE TRIPPIN

Anyway, Alvin had been a metro-city bus driver for more than twenty years and knew all the city streets, back-alleys, short-cuts, and where all the major potholes where like he knew the back of his hand. But he still had one vice—listening to James Brown while he was driving. He put on his music to drown out everything and everybody around him. Listening to James Brown was the stimulus that aroused his soul and enabled him to 'Get on the Good-Foot,' that is to say; the music triggered his reckless style of driving.

The task ahead for Alvin was a big one. He had to make several more stops until he picked up everyone on his list. That meant traveling from one neighborhood to another all around the city.

With that being the case, he buckled his seat belt, popped the clutch, and took off like he was coming out of a pit-stop at the Indy-500. He drove up the street, around the corner, and down to the bottom of Sheffield Road in record timing.

When he reached the bottom, there was a 25mph speed limit sign, so he came to a complete stop to observe the landscape. There was a long winding road ahead of him with fenced-in pastureland on both sides of the road. The reason for the fence was because a lot of times there where a dozen or so head of cattle grazing in the pasture, and sometimes they'd get spooked by the sound of loud cars and trucks passing by and go astray. At times they'd trample over the fence and wind up on the road. What's worse is that on this particular morning, there was a thick fog hovering over the road ahead.

Well, as expected, he took off like a kamikaze pilot on a suicide mission. He got a little further down the road and spotted a cow in the middle of the fog filled road; then another, and another. And despite their fear, protesting, and hollering at him to not do what he was obviously about to do, it was worthless. He had those headphones on his head, and all he could hear was James Brown hollering and screaming in his ears; he couldn't hear a word they were saying. Hearing James Brown was all that mattered to him.

So, he turned on his bright lights, blew his horn, and with his mind being completely absorbed with the thought of completing the mission he had set out to do. He put his foot on the gas and kept on driving like a mad man. These kids had no choice other than to respond in unison with a long, drawn-out: AWE......................SHIT!

He zig-zagged his way through a mile long stretch of cows and cow manure in less than 60 seconds. He swerved left in front of the first cow and grazed its jaw making it turn around and go back to the field that it came from. He broke to the right of the second cow and ran over a huge pile of cow manure. All of a sudden, the rear end of the bus fishtailed one-way then the other, and it just so happened that the back end of the bus smacked a cow on its rear end and pushed it across the road into the field on the other side.

Several yards later he saw two more cows crossing the road. One was behind the other, with about three yards between them, and he immediately mashed on the accelerator and shot right between them like he was in a demolition derby. The two cows scampered away in different directions only to wind up falling over in the ditches on the sides of the road.

Then he got to a bend in the road and couldn't see around the corner. There was a cow standing in the middle of the road. It was mooing and it seemed to be mesmerized by the sound of the bus engine and the oncoming light in the road. Alvin slowed down a little, but he was still traveling a little too fast when he saw the cow standing there. He quickly hit the breaks to avoid hitting it, but by now his front and back tires were covered with cow manure and the bus skidded several feet before Alvin could get control of it, and as a result, the bus went into a 360-degree flat spin. Bodies pummeled and tumbled from one side of the bus to the other; they spent completely around in a circle in the middle of the road before they came to a stop.

After they stopped spinning, Alvin got his bearings together and made a U-Turn. He drove off the road into the grass. Then he drove right past the cow that was miraculously still standing in the same spot and got back on the road.

Well, when they finally reached the end of the road, there was a sigh of relief. These Holy Crusaders had made it. But there were a few more stops to make before they reached their final destination—the Clifton Ave. Church. Furthermore, they were all seriously wondering if they'd make it to the church before they met their maker.

CONTINUED

At the intersection of the main road, they made a right turn and rode a half mile to the first light. Then they made a left turn onto route 42 and followed it down a hill—up a hill—and down another hill until they reached the I-75 entrance ramp and merged into the highway traffic. Not more than three minutes later they got off at the Lincoln Heights exit and went straight to big mama's house. Their where three more cousins *there waiting: Leroy, Sparkle, and Leon.*

Leon alone was a nerve-racking nuisance. Linda, who was also Leon's Aunt, had to deal with the day-to-day problems that he created. He stayed high smoking weed 24-7. Furthermore, she was desperately trying to keep Leroy from going to jail from selling crack, and from hanging around the demented drug hustlers in the neighborhood. Then there was, Sparkle. Keeping her away from a fast girls, who would do any and everything to get hold of some money was a major concern of hers. Other than that, keeping a steady job and enough food in the house was hard enough to do.

Anyway, after Alvin picked them up, he drove to the upper sub to pick up cousins, Lee, his sister, Lavada, and his favorite cousin, Little Gary—aka-Popsicle. But when he got there, he took a short ride through the hood to see how much things had changed and, he encountered several amusing situations.

The first thing he saw was a group of angry people shouting and cursing at the police. They were calling the police a bunch of no-good ass crooks on the take. Alvin had heard those kinds of insults before, so he kept right on driving, and said to himself (some shit never changes). It was a regular routine for dirty cops to harass the dope boy's and take their drugs and money. Then they'd lock them up overnight and let them go in the morning. The routine happened so much that the cops started getting high on the drugs they confiscated from the dope-boys, and as quiet as it was kept, selling more drugs than the dope-boys.

As he drove further up the street, and before he could turn the corner he almost ran into an old wino. The man walked out in the middle of the street and forced Alvin to make a sudden stop. After he stopped, the man started banging on the hood of the bus and shouting: "What's my name, God-dammit." He stood there mumbling with his body weaving back and forth, shouting the same thing over and over. Then he stared inside the bus with a frightful look on his face. When Alvin recognized the man, he got off the bus and talked to him for a few seconds, then he helped the man to the curb and had him sit down. Then Alvin stuck a few dollars in his shirt pocket and left him sitting of the curb.

It's a sad story, but Macon Lacky was a brilliant brick mason back in his day. He had built nursing homes and houses throughout the city, but for some reason he lost his mind. He started destroying his own work with home-made bombs, and by setting fires to the places he built.

Anyway, after that. Alvin drove midways down the hill to the Valley Homes--the projects where Popsicle lived. As soon as they turned the corner, there he was—the cherry-lipped bandit. Alvin spotted him from the street. He was down on his knees in the parking lot shaking a pair of dice. He got the nick name Popsicle because when he was a young child, his mother spoiled him rotten. Every time she took him to the store he'd beg, cry, wine, and demand his mother to buy him a Popsicle. If she didn't, he'd pitch a bitch-fit, and lay down in the middle of the floor kicking and crying until she, or someone did. Sometimes complete strangers would offer to buy him a popsicle to shut him up.

Alvin pulled in the parking lot and saw him in a crap game with five older boys. He was in the middle, down on a knee with his hand raised in the air shaking a pair of dice, swearing to send all of them home broke. But, when he threw the dice, they landed, and his heart sunk. "Snake eyes, sorry little nigga, you lose!" the boys laughed at him and teased him relentlessly. They told him to: "take your young, broke black-ass home, and don't go away mad, just go the fuck away—you little bastard!"

Popsicle was pissed in more ways than one. He had just lost all his money, and he learned a lesson in humility from those boys that sure as hell didn't help his self-esteem.

But, if you knew Popsicle, you would have known the he was going to change the way things turned out, and there couldn't have been a better time for Popsicle to pull off what he did next. Popsicle went into a tirade and started cussing and fussing at everybody around him. He went wild-- jumping up and down on top of the money and kicking it all around. They all thought he had lost his mind. But his next move was unbelievable. All of a sudden, he fell down on top of the money, and before he got up, he grabbed a hand full of money and stampeded though those older boys like he was a candidate for the Heisman trophy.

Alvin had just turned the bus around and was headed back out the parking lot when he saw Popsicle kicking up rocks and gravel running away from the gang of boys. All of a sudden, one of the boys caught up with Popsicle and grabbed him by his shirt collar. He was holding on to him, but Popsicle changed gears on the boy, he got down low and flew straight out of his shirt and kept on trucking. Shortly after that, Alvin opened the bus doors and

Popsicle made a leaping dive. He looked like a tailback making an end zone touchdown, and he wound up landing across Alvin's lap.

Alvin's timing was perfect. He pulled the door shut, but those boys were still running alongside the bus--banging on the door trying to pry it open. It didn't matter though because, Alvin went to work putting his years of driving skills to good use. He mashed the gas pedal to the floor and made an impossible 45 degree turn out of that parking lot. He was traveling so fast, and his turn out of the parking lot was so sharp, that the bus tilted on its two side tires going around the corner.

They got away, but not before the back of bus was bombarded with rocks, bottles. sticks, and anything those pissed off boys could find to throw at it. Everyone on the bus was terrified. Everyone except Popsicle. He was happier than a convict that just made parole. He had just escaped another beat-down. That being the case, he ran to the back of the bus and taunted the boys through the rear window. They couldn't hear him, but they sure as hell knew what he was saying. "Yall some Busters, you can't catch me, Yall some chumps!" Then he did the cabbage patch--pause from time to time to blurt out: "You Can't Touch This."

Well, Despite the jeopardizing situation Popsicle put them through, Alvin had one more stop to make in this wacked out neighborhood, and he knew it would have to be a quick one. He drove back to the upper sub to pick up Big Lee and Lavada. He was right in the nick of time too. They were more than ready to go. The next-door neighbor had just called the police because of the noise coming from their house. Lee had just kicked off in his stepdaddy ass because his mother had another black eye. Every time his stepfather came home drunk, he'd get into a fight with his mother. He was tired of seeing him terrorize his baby sister too. He couldn't take any more of his stepfather's shit. The hostility he had towards him came to a boiling point and he exploded. They were ready to go with their bags packed as soon as Alvin drove up.

Alvin fled from the scene just as the police were arriving. He eventually got back on the freeway and headed straight to his sister Lorraine's house. After he got off the freeway, he stopped at the red light at the intersection. But when he took off again, they heard something tapping at the back of the bus. Alvin looked through the side view mirror and saw his bald, melon head nephew on his bicycle in the middle of the street hanging onto the side of the bus.

Monty was up to his dangerous games again, and not only did he get their attention, he got the attention of the semi-truck driver in the left lane coming straight towards him. The driver didn't have much time to make a complete stop, so he started blowing his horn from a block away. All of a sudden, Alvin decided to speed up and make a right turn instead of going straight. A split second later, Monty grabbed hold of the bus and followed it out of the path of the oncoming truck, but little did he know that his mother almost had a heart attack watching the whole incident from her porch on the next street.

It was a close a call for, Monty, because if Alvin hadn't made that right turn, he would have wound up lying next to a grease spot in the middle of rode, and there was no doubt in his mother's mind, that she was going to turn the benefit of him having that good luck into an ass whooping when he got home.

Start.

When the bus pulled in the yard, Monty was right behind it.

When his mother spotted him, she immediately did a two -handed vault off the front porch railing and landed in the front yard. Then she went straight to where he was standing. He was laughing and joking with Earlene and A.J. through the bus window, and when he turned around, she shocked the shit out of him. She immediately started beating him with the hard rubber house slipper she had pulled off her foot.

Monty tried to bob and weave and cover up from the stinging blows. She hit him upside his head and on every part of his body she could get to. She was too mad, and too fast with that slipper to let any open area on his body go unpunished.

The kids on the bus started out feeling sorry for him when they saw the merciless beating he was getting. They cringed and squinting their eyes every time they heard the sound of those smacks to his body. But, what came out of his mouth next changed all of that.

After what seemed like an eternity of smacks upside his head, Monty made the mistake of calling his mother the "B" word. He must have been delirious from the ass whooping she was putting on him, and he was so fed up with the licks to his body that he shouted: "Stop hitting me bitch!" Well, that didn't do any good because the sympathy they once had for him turned into instructions on how to beat his ass.

A.J. Hollered out the bus window, "Hit his ass again, Aunt Lorraine, show him what ya working with."

Earlene Hollered, "Yeah, hit that fool again, Aunt Lorraine. Knock the meat off his ass! He needs his ass whooped!"

D.A. said: "Yeah, use a night-stick on his Ass."

Danielle said: "Yeah, knock the taste out of his mouth, Aunt Lorraine. He ain't got no business cussing you."

When Sam and Sparkle heard what they were saying, they got in on the act, and both of them shouted out the window at the same time, "Yeah, Kick his ass."

Leon heard everything they said and couldn't think of a thing to say.

So, he stood up and hollered out the window: "Yeah, what they said, and started laughing, Ehee, hee hee hee hee hee...."

Anyway, right after that devastating beat-down, they gathered up what was left of Monty, got him on the bus, and continued the mission. This time, instead of getting on the highway, Alvin took a shortcut. He went straight down Paddock Road, which took him about ten minutes to get to sister, Norlene's house. When he got there, he'd pick up big Kim, Ernie, and baby sister, Angie.

When he pulled up, they were standing at the door—well dressed, looking sophisticated, and ready to go. So, knowing that Alvin was pressed for time, they said good-bye to their parents and got on the bus without delay.

Well, Alvin had one more stop to make before he could start heading for the church. That stop was the Greyhound station downtown. Little Walter--aka-Chunk, was riding the bus up from Atlanta, and Hopefully he'd be there right on time to pick him up, and he was. The bus had just dropped him off.

From there, they traveled West through a downtown portion of the city to Vine Street. They made a right turn and went up Vine to Mulberry—one of the steepest hills in the city. It took a while with the bus filled to capacity and luggage everywhere, but that yellow, rusty little jitney performed like "The little engine that could." It smoked, choked, stuttered, puttered and backfired until it made it to the top of the hill to the church.

CHAPTER FIVE

A TASTE OF HOLINESS

When they pulled up, Aunt Ella was on the church steps standing tall and gleaming with pride. But she was shocked to see what happened next. As soon as all the kids were the off the bus, Alvin pulled off to park. When he did, it sounded like gunfire. There was a loud Boom, bang and popping noises. The exhaust system backfired, and all of them hit the ground like they were in a war zone.

Aunt Ella was as stunned, as were the other church members standing outside when they saw their reaction to the noise. But, Aunt Ella understood why they reacted the way they did, and she calmly told them to: "get up off the ground, ain't nobody shooting at y'all.". Afterwards, she had them inside the church sitting in the front section of pews that she reserved for her family.

Meanwhile, the noise in the church had reached its peak; chatter and bantering filled the room. When Reverend Kimble made it to the pulpit to welcome everybody, he rapped on the microphone a few times to get their attention, and to quiet them down, he spoke to the church loud and clear and said:

"Can everybody say, Amen?"

The church said: "Amen!"

"I said, can everybody say, Amen!"

"Amen, Reverend; Amen, Amen..."

"Hallelujah! Praise the Lord! I see the glory of the Lord in church this morning. Oh, Happy Day! I see the Johnson family here. The Thomas family—Alberta and Calvin and their lovely children, praise the lord, and Sister Walker—my, my, my, it looks like Sister Walker brought her entire family here this morning. Praise the Lord. I see your son Alvin and his children, and I see your other Grandchildren. And these other children must be your brother and sister's, children."

"They're my Great-nieces and nephews Reverend" she said proudly. "Have Mercy, Sister Walker, you must be a Shepherd for the Lord! Yes, truly a Shepherd for the Lord. Everybody, give Sister Walker a round of applauds, Amen."

Well, this was the point when these kids started getting restless. They had been quiet and peaceful up until now, but now they had no interest in what Reverend Kimble was saying. Their interest was on other things; mainly in observing members of the opposite sex and cracking jokes about the church members. Furthermore, listening to Sister Althea speak bored them to the end of their wits. By now they had gotten hot and thirsty, and their backsides were hurting from sitting on those hard, wooden pews. They were ready to get up and bust a move, or do something.

Fortunately, relief came just in time. After Sister Althea finished her announcements, they all broke up into Sunday school groups. They dispersed upstairs and downstairs to the basement. Tables and chairs were being set up in the basement, and the number of groups were being determined by the deacons and the elders in the church. So, after a few minutes of decision making were made, as to who and how many people would be in the groups, everybody went to their assigned Sunday school teacher.

Well, as it turned out, five-rambling-rascals were in one group. They included: A. J., D. A., Leon, Popsicle, and Monty. Walter, Ernie, and Leroy and a few other kids were in another.

The girl groups included: Earlene, Samantha, Danielle, Lavada, and Sparkle--all in the same group. Big Kim, Angie, and Tamara were upstairs in another group.

Furthermore, there were so many people in attendance that week that Reverend Kimble had, Peaches, his daughter, take charge of teaching one of the groups, and it happened to be the one with the five Rambling Rascals in it. In addition to them being in the same group, twin sisters, Jeanie and Janie were in it. The rascals gave them the name the 'X-ray vision sisters' because of the thickness of the lens in their glasses. Then there was a boy named, Antoine. They called him 'Precious,' because of the feminine sound of his voice.

Anyway, with the group being under control, so far, Peaches started her lesson with the story about Jonah and the Whale.

The group with Ernie, Walter, Leroy, and five sassy, snobbish acting girls in it was being taught by Sister Althea--the Reverend's wife. She was a nice-looking woman in her mid-fifties, but she was a stern, uncompromising woman who demanded respect. Her lesson was about, Job.

Next, there was Deacon Brown--an elderly man in his eighties. He was the mentor in charge of the group with Earlene, Samantha, Danielle, Lavada, and Sparkle in it. These girls were sitting in a circle next to four boys. They had a funky smell about them that literally made them sick. They stunk in every way imaginable. They had bad breath, stinking underarms, and the clothes they wore clothes smelled like they came a off garbage truck. Deacon Brown didn't know it at the time, but he was going to have his hands full with this group; it was just a matter of time before the spontaneous combustion that this group created, lit up like fireworks. Their lesson was the story of Sampson and Delilah.

Big Kim, Angie, and Tamara were in a group with some girls whose understanding of the Bible had a whole different understanding than theirs. There was a combination of righteous indignation and contempt between them about religious issues. This brought out the worse in these girls; and as a result, their disagreements created a 'Bible Thumping Calamity'. Their mentor, Sister Pauline did her best to maintain peace and order between the girls; however, she didn't want to take sides, but she knew that some of the girls conception of the actual Bible scriptures had been misconstrued. Their lesson was about the Descendants of Abraham.

START.

Nonetheless, Peaches had started telling her group the story of Jonah. She got to the part about the men on the ship tossing Jonah in the sea, because of a curse that was thought to be on him, and him being swallowed by a whale, she was doing good. But unfortunately, when she added the part about him living for three days inside the whale's belly, it was too hard of a story for the Rambling Rascals to swallow. So, with them being the smart asses they were-- they questioned and criticized her information: (How could a man be swallowed by a whale and come out alive three days later?). And as such, it was the natural disbelief in their minds that set their imaginations on a course of ridiculous questions, comments, and jokes. Throughout her lesson, there was an inquisition of ludicrous questions and answers among them.

Monty: " Hey A.J., what would you do if you got swallowed by a whale?"

A.J.: "man, if a whale swallowed me, I'd pull out my nine and shoot that mother-fucker it's ass until it opened up its mouth and let me out."

What about you, D.A.: "If a whale swallowed me, I'd start cooking his ass from the inside out. And when it's done, I'd put some hot sauce on it and eat me a big ass fish sandwich."

Monty: "Yeah man, but then you'd need is some coleslaw and a bottle of coke to go with it?"

What about you, Popsicle: "Popsicle put his hand in his back pocket and pulled out his knife and said, I'd Fillet his ass. He'd be fried, died, and laid to the side when I'm through him. "The only thing I'd want is a coke and some fries."

Right after he said that, Leon couldn't help but to blurted out: "Yeah, and some ketchup. Eeeh-hee hee.... Eeeh-hee hee...!"

Twin sisters, Jeanie and Janie had heard the story of Jonah before, and they tried to tell them about the meaning in it, but they got shot down every time they tried. They wasted their time trying to explain the lesson in the story to those nuts. But Antoine, he just sat there quietly shaking his head back and forth in disbelief. He wasn't about to say a word in favor of or against the discussion.

During the interim, and from the corner of his eye, Ernie could see that Peaches was struggling with the nonsense that his cousins were taking her through. Occasionally she caught a glimpse of him watching her, but the only way she communicate with him was with the excruciating smile on her face. Anyway, Peaches continued to tell the story with Jeanie, Janie, and Antoine being her only listening pupils.

Nonetheless, as time went by, A.J. noticed Antoine staring at the ceiling with a smile on his face, and A.J. was curious about what he was looking at and why he was smiling. So, he asked Antoine where his mind was, and what was he looking at. But Antoine, still smiling and looking at the ceiling nonchalantly answered him in his soft, feminine voice "Oh nothing."

Well, Popsicle was wondering the same thing. So, he sat down next to Antoine and stared at him for a long, hard minute or two. Then he looked up at the ceiling where Antoine was looking, then back at Antoine. Then he turned back around toward the rest of the boys and surmised an assumption. He said: "I don't know what he's looking at, but he's got that 'I want to suck Moby Dick's, Dick look in his eye if you ask me.' D.A. immediately responded by saying: "You better let him use your knife then, Pop. He's gonna have to cut both corners of his mouth to get that big mutha-fucka in it!" Leon couldn't stop laughing when D.A. said that--Eeeh-he ...!"

Nonetheless, Sister Althea's group got along fine. She found out that Ernie was a well-versed student of Bible scripture, and halfway through the lesson she let him take control of the group-- he told the story of Job, and explained to the rest of the group that: "The Devil told God that Job would lose all him faith in him if all his wealth was taken away. "So, God let the Devil test Job to prove his loyalty. He let the Devil take everything from Job--his wealth, worldly possessions, and his family. However, Job proved his loyalty and faith in God even when all of his wealth, worldly possessions, and his family was taken away. So, it turned out that the devil lost the bet, and God blessed Job with twice as much as he had before, and he lived to be a hundred and forty years old."

Well, Lee was listening, and he figured out the meaning behind the story. He said, "I see. It was a test of Faith. Job may have lost a lot, but in the end, he gained a whole lot more because he never gave up his faith in God."

But, on the other hand, Chunk's visionary knowledge about the story was somewhere else. The first thought that crossed his mind was that God and the Devil were a couple of gamblers betting on a card game of chances. And for some reason, Leroy could care less. His mind was on making money, and making money was all that was on his mind. He just wanted to get the Hell out of there.

Anyway, as the discussions progressed, and at times digressed from the intended lesson, the Rambling Rascals were wandering off—one by one. They were going to the bathroom and disappearing out the basement door. And, with less tension to deal with, Peaches was relieved when she saw them leaving; she didn't care at all. There was less confusion in the group and it was a lot easier to manage; however, during the next ten minutes, she looked around and all five of them were gone.

All of them followed the same escape route. They went to the bathroom and then out the basement door next to the kitchen. Then they went up a long flight of steps to the front of the church, and down the hill to the store on the corner where they all met.

This was A.J.'s regular route when he went to church with his Grandma. Whenever he got bored, he'd slip away and run down the hill to the store. Anyway, A.J. had been sitting in the same spot for several minutes before the other boys showed up, and when they all made it, it wasn't long before they decided to venture across the downtown intersection and head toward the West End.

Strangely, it just so happened that the further they walked, the more they got a feeling that someone was watching them, or that there was some sort invisible force field around them. All in all, they felt like they were invincible; they strutted through the side alleys and streets downtown like they owned them.

A few minutes later, they were in Washington Park. When they got there, they saw people sleeping on benches; on the top of cardboard boxes, and some were walking around aimlessly. Some of the teens had a game of basketball going on while others watched from the side of the courts. Across the street, there were winos and drug addicts hanging out in front of the neighborhood pony keg panhandling.

Further on up the street, the drop-in center had just put a bunch of people out so they could clean up and sanitized the bedding area; a lot of them would wind up in a crap game in the alley, or turn up shot, stabbed to dead.

Meanwhile, back at the church, Aunt Ella and her peers, Sister Wilson, Deacon Bradley, and Reverend Kimble were engaged in a heated discussion that had little, and everything to do with church. They talked about the lack of respect kids today had for their family, for themselves, and other people. They also talked about the disproportionate number of young black men in jail, the growing number of teenage girls getting pregnant, and the increasing number of high school drop outs.

Surprisingly, Sister Althea's group strayed away from the Bible study subject about 'Job. Lee, Ernie, Walter, Leroy, and the rest of the group, including Sister Althea, wound up talking about food, sports, and the opposite sex.

Peaches and her group were getting along fine now that she didn't have to put up with the 'mod squad.' She reported them MIA to the head Deacon about a half hour earlier, but she had serious doubts about them doing anything about it. And with time ticking away, Sunday school was about over. Reverend Kimble was preparing for his sermon as well as anticipating the donations from the circulation of the collection plate. Other than that, the only concerns at that time were with some of the girls.

Earlene and Danielle were getting pissed off with the disrespect and foul language coming out of the mouths of the boys in their group. The story of Sampson and Delilah was the Bible lesson in their study group, but their real problem boiled down to the boys defending Sampson and dishing, Delilah. The boys despised Delilah, and it became apparent from the language they used to describe her. But every time they said something disrespectful about, Delilah they would look right at the girls when they said it. So, the girls took it as a personal assault against them. Naturally, they felt compelled to do something about it; so they swore that the next time they called Delilah out of her name--Shit was going to hit the fan.

In addition, the group's mentor, 80- year- old Deacon Brown was hard of hearing, and at times he suffered from a mild case of dementia. His memory would come and go, and some of the words he heard were hard for him to discern. So, with that being the case, these boys exploited the fact of his illness and got away with calling Delilah vulgar names such as: (a medieval prostitute, an ancient Hoe, and a back-stabbing bitch).

Well, as it turned out, they continued taking turns reading the story out loud and the boys started talking about Delilah again. This time one of the boys was looking straight at Earlene when he called Delilah a (Rotten Ass Bitch), and before he could get another word out, Earlene jumped up and cold-cocked him in his mouth. He obviously went down for the count, but Earlene was still on top of him hollering: "Your Mama's a Rotten Bitch! You stinky-ass little boy!" Then she sat on him and knocked his head from east to west with right and left hooks.

Fortunately, Deacon Brown glanced over and saw them on the floor in a brawl and snapped back to reality. It took Deacon Brown with the help of Danielle and Samantha to pull her off of him. And right after the fight was over, Deacon Brown nervously fumbled through his jacket pocket to find his pills. He quickly swallowed one, and without thinking about where he was, he shouted: "I am too Damn Old for this Shit!" After that, the girls were sent back upstairs to be under Aunt Ella's supervision.

Back in Washington Park, trouble was on the front line for these boys, and there was a clear element of danger ahead of them. However, regardless of that being the case, these boys still found things in common with the people around them.

D. A. was interested in the basketball game that was going on in the park, and a when he had a chance to play, he showed off his prowess. Although he was good and knew it, he was also a ball hog and he tended to piss-off his teammates as well as his opponents.

As for Popsicle, It was just a matter of time before he heard the hustle and bustle of a crap game going on in the alley. His natural instincts led that money hungry, cash-grabbing, get bad ass, to a game in the alley; he got spot in a game and lost his last few dollars.

A J's desire to borrow other people's property without permission hadn't changed a bit. For some reason, he was obsessed with taking other people's bicycles, and it really didn't matter who it belonged to. So, it wasn't surprising when he saw an abandoned ten-speed laying in front of the corner pony keg, that this natural instinct would tell him to take, break, and roll; he got on it and hit the wind.

Monty and Leon had other ideas about how to enjoy their escape from church, so they did what came naturally. They followed the smell of weed behind the store. When they met up with the pot-heads smoking it, they put their change together and got one of the locals to buy them a fifth of wine. After that, it was share and share alike. They passed their wine, and the local boys passed their weed. They got their swerve on, and it didn't take long for them to wind up looking slack-eyed, silly, and talking shit.

Well to sum up this little adventure, Popsicle wound up losing all of his money in the crap game, which resulted in him getting pissed off and talking shit. D.A showboated in the basketball game he was in and pissed the other team off by hustling them out of their money. A.J. jacked a bicycle and went on a sightseeing trip all over the city. And Monty and Leon got so high on drinking wine and smoking pot that they couldn't tell the difference between shoe polish and shit. But their short adventure was about to come to an end.

As things turned out, the tension in the neighborhood was getting thick, and a lot of attitudes were changing. To put it plain, the level of unrest from some of the residents in the community was coming to a climax.

Two Cincinnati cop cars pulled up and stopped at the corner of Race and 13th street. They got a complaint about a stolen ten-speed bicycle. The mother of the boy whose bike was missing called the police and gave them a description of the stolen bike. There were no witnesses to identify the thief who took it, but it didn't take long for someone who knew A.J. to spot him riding it through the city. As a matter of fact, the boy that spotted him happened to be the boy's cousin. Furthermore, the worse part about it was that the boy was a member of a notorious gang called the 'Tot-Lot-Posses'.

Meanwhile, during this time span, once again, turmoil was on the rise at the church. There was a difference in the points of view about the Bible scripture regarding the Prophet Abraham. Some of the girls contested the fact that Joseph was born through the bloodline of Isaac. Kim, Angie, and Tamara were all arguing that he was. Moreover, they were fed up with the idiotic way of thinking the other group of girls had.

As a result, one stupid comment led to another, until finally, these girls set-it-off. They stood face to face in a shouting match arguing their point, and when no neutral ground could be gained, they started hurling insults at each other:

(Marlene) "Kim, you're stupid, your mama must have dropped you on your head when you were born. You don't know what you're talking about"

(Kim) "Wait a minute, Heifer! You're the one who's stupid. That's why you had to stay in the second grade for three years.

(Marlene) "Girl, don't talk about your mama like that!"

(Kim) "Ah girl, your mama had to slap the ugly off you when you was born just to get your own dog to play with you."

(Marlene) "Girl-friend, your mama's a alcoholic. She drank so much that she ran the corner liquor store out of business."

(Kim) "Awe bitch, your mama's so Butch that a talent scout signed her to a contract to play fullback for the hefty Ho's!"

(Marlene) "Wait a minute, Bitch! Don't be talking about my mama!"

(Kim) "Okay, I'll talk about your daddy then. Your daddy is so tight with his money that his ass squeaks when he walks. You didn't get your first pair of shoes until you were 11 years old."

(Marlene) "Awe girl, your daddy looks like he got shot in the face with a Shit-Gun."

(Kim) "Ah Bitch! your faggot ass daddy can suck a dick longer than a flashlight shining through the back end of a school bus."

"You Fat Heifer!"

"You Black Bitch!"

In the split second that followed, Marlene caught Kim by surprise with a swung on her with a right hook that barely missed because no sooner than she swung Kim faded back to miss the swing and was quick to come back with an overhand right and hit Marlene square in her jaw. Marlene back peddled, lost her balance, and wound up in a row of pews behind her. Then, with Marlene out of commission, her sister, Mary stepped in to retaliate. She grabbed Kim by the hair and pulled off her wig. So, she flung it in the air and charged Kim like a mad bull.

But Angie was quick to stick her foot out and trip her when she charged. She fell to the floor, and Angie jumped on her back, grabbed a Bible from the pew, and started beating her in the back of her head with it. After that, Tamara wound up squaring off with the oldest sister, Marsha. They went to knuckle city--looking like two heavy-weight boxers. They sparred for a while, then they locked heads and fell to the floor rocking and rolling in the middle of the church aisle. But after a few minutes, it finally came to an end when Alvin and a couple of the Deacons broke them up.

Their Grandma Ella didn't know what to do about these girls. She had just been through the same kind of drama with the other girls, and she was really getting frustrated with the lot of them. But for some reason, she didn't let it bother her. Instead, she took this as a sign from above and prayed about it. She asked the lord to forgive them, and prayed for them right there in the church.

Meanwhile, back in the hood, a couple of the police officers decided to take a walkthrough Washington Park. They asked different people questions about the bicycle theft. They went to the corner stores and randomly checked for I.D.'s. So, when the cops finally got to Monty and Leon, they were higher than two kites in a windstorm.

"Hey, Shit for brains, come here--you to scum bag! Did either one of you boys see anybody riding around on a new ten-speed bicycle this morning?" Monty said "No sir officer sir. Swear to God! Shit, I thought I was blind till I seent you walk up here, ain't that right, Leon. "Yeah, That's Right, we blind, we ain't seent Shit!"

Well, the cops couldn't argue with that, and they couldn't do anything about it. All they did was look at them like they were a couple of jackasses, and tell them to get the hell away from there; anything else would have been a waste of time. And thank God they were smart enough to disappear through the next alley they saw and head back to the church.

As for D. A., he felt the animosity building up in the teams he and his crew were beating, so he decided to cut his last game short because of the anger that was brewing. He and his two-man crew had already won five out of five games--at five dollars a game, and likewise, some of the downtown street-ballers were pissed off because they couldn't stop him from scoring, so, they got mad and started fouling him.

But he had already gotten what he came for, and when he looked over and saw the police asking Monty and Leon questions, he got wise and decided to shake and break back to the church too. It was just a few minutes later before he caught up with Monty and Leon.

And as for Popsicle, his luck had run out and he was down to his last dollar. So, when he saw the cops patrolling the streets, he saw a natural opportunity come into view. He knew all too well what to do, and how to do it because he had been in this same situation before. That being the case, he went into his bag of tricks and used the element of misdirection to get out of this situation and make a cash grab.

On his turn to throw the dice, he recklessly overthrew them to the far side of the alley, and while everybody was looking for the dice, he stood up and shouted: "Here Comes Five-0! Here Comes Five -0!" And the split second that everyone looked up the alley in the same direction, it was the same split second that he grabbed a fist full of money off the ground, and took off running down the alley in the opposite direction.

It was unbelievable, and an amazing to sight to see how fast that boy could run. When those wine heads and thugs took off after him, you could tell from watching that they'd never catch him. Popsicle took off like a runaway slave with a gang of bloodhounds on his ass.

When he got to the next street, some of those thugs were still chasing him, and that's Popsicle went into high gear--hitting every gear in between. A few seconds later, he saw A.J. riding on that bicycle on the next street--right up ahead of him. So, he caught up with him and was running right beside him. But when he heard the footsteps coming up behind him, he waved goodbye to A.J. and ran right past him.

When A.J. heard the footsteps behind him, he looked back and saw the gang of thugs, and figured that they must be after Popsicle. But, by now, Popsicle had put so much distance between them that they just gave up.

After they gave up, A.J. quickly sped up to catch up with Popsicle, and as soon as he did, one of the gang members from the Tot-Lot-Posse spotted him and pointed him out as the thief that stole his cousin's bike.

Well, a few ticks later, they all met up at the bottom corner of the intersection. A.J., D. A., Monty, Leon, and Popsicle were all there with two blocks, and a steep hill to tackle before they reached the church.

But suddenly, from a distance, they heard the sound of angry voices coming from the playground on the next corner. They turned to look and saw one of the boys pointing his finger at them saying: "There's the motherfucker that stole my cousin's bike!" Another guy asked: "Who are those niggas?" And another one said, "They ain't from around here." Well, with that being said they all recited the gang slogan: "Pins and needles, needles and pins: a dead nigga is a nigga that don't grin!"

After that, twenty gang members were walking toward them fast, fast, fast. However, by the time the rest of the boys figured out what was going on, A.J. had taken off across the street on that bike and was headed up the hill. With that being the case, one of the gang members spotted him on the bike and fired his pistol at him. When the other boys heard the shots, they stormed up that hill like soldiers on a beach front--scared to death.

But not long after A.J. busted his move, a miraculous event occurred. A.J. made it to the second block and was about to turn the corner and go up the hill. But, when he got to the corner, he saw a ghostly apparition standing there.

It stood over seven feet tall. It had a black hood covering its head and face; and it was holding a long, thick wooden staff in its hand.

When he got closer, the apparition banged the staff on the ground. It sounded like thunder, and it shook the ground so hard that the bicycle stood straight up on its back wheel-- A.J. fell off and hit the ground. He couldn't believe what had just happened, but he didn't have time to think about it either—he looked back, then forward, and kept on running as fast as he could up that hill to the church.

When the rest of the boys reached the corner, they saw the seven-foot, hooded apparition on the corner as well, but their attention span and their ears were more in tune to the sound of the footsteps they heard behind them and the sound of the bullets whizzing over their heads.

Likewise, they turned the corner and ran up that hill right behind A.J. As they were doing so, they heard that thunderous bang again, they looked back and an even more miraculous was seeing that ghostly apparition stand out on the sidewalk, open its arms, and from out of nowhere, a strong gust of wind came and blew those gang members, and the bicycle back down the hill and across the intersection.

When they made it to the church, they opened the doors and ran inside huffing, and puffing; they were out of breath but relieved to still be alive.

But, the good part about their adventure was that they came back right on time for Sunday Service. Everyone was in the process of convening upstairs for the sermon. And for some reason, instead of viewing these boys as missing in action from Sunday school service, their sudden and timely presence busting through the front doors of the church was looked at like their eagerness to hear lessons about the Lord.

CHAPTER SIX
HOLY HYPNOSIS

The people were settling down in their seats when Reverend Kimble approached the pulpit to bless the congregation with a prayer. After that he announced the topic of the day's sermon. But before he gave the sermon, the ushers passed around collection plates for church donations while the choir backed up an out-of-town guest singing a gospel song.

> Master, the tempest is raging
> The billows are tossing high.
> The sky is o'er shadowed with
> Blackness
> No shelter or help is nigh.
> Carest Thou not that we perish?
> How canst Thou lie asleep
> When each moment so madly
> is threatening
> A grave in the angry deep
> The winds and the waves shall
> obey my will, peace be still.
> Whether the wrath of the
> storm-tossed sea
> Or demons or men or
> whatever it be
> No water can swallow the ship
> where lies
> The Master of ocean and earth
> and skies
> They shall sweetly obey my will
> Peace be still, peace be still
> They all shall sweetly obey my
> will, peace be still, peace be still.
> When you're burdened: Peace

> When you're lonely: Peace
>
> When you're hungry: Peace

Following the end of the song, Reverend Kimble returned to the pulpit. However, as soon as he opened his mouth to speak, he was silenced by the loud sound of thunder that echoed through the church; the entire church congregation looked to the back, and then to the front of the church. No-one knew where the noise came from. Then they were blinded by a bright light that swept through the church and lasted all but a split second.

But, after their vision cleared, they regained their sight and saw an enormously tall figure of someone or something standing at the pulpit next to Reverend Kimble. Whoever it was, or whatever it was wore a long, black and gold hooded robe, and it wielded a long, thick, black wooden staff.

After it removed its hood, a gasping sound of fear from disbelief filled the room. They couldn't tell if it was a man or a women, but it resembled the likes of a mythological creature from the past. It had bird-like facial features that resembled an eagle and it glistened like a piece of shiny coal. Its eyes were dark and piercing like an eagle's, and it was wearing a solid white ivory necklace around its neck. But even more chilling was the sound of its deep-dry gravelly voice when it spoke.

"JAMBO, WATU WASURI—GREETINGS, BEAUTIFUL PEOPLE

I HAVE BEEN WATCHING YOU.

I AM THE JAMACAN PRIESTESS MAMA CREO-LARD.

I HAVE BEEN SENT FROM THE AFTER WORLD TO BRING YOU A MESSAGE OF LIFE.

PROTECT YOUR CHILDREN.

PROTECT YOUR CHILDREN FROM THE (SEEDS OF TEMPTATION). PROTECT YOUR CHILDREN'S CHILDREN

SO THAT THEY MAY MULITPLE IN BEAUTY,

AND MULTIPLY THE BEAUTY OF THE EARTH.

LIFE IS A PRECIOUS STEPINGSTONE.

USE IT TO ATTAIN A GLORIOUS DEATH.

THERE IS EVERLASTING LIFE IN THE AFTER WORLD.

IT HAS BEEN ORDAINED BY JAH ON THIS EARTH,

IT IS JAH'S WILL THAT IT BE DONE."

"NOW, BEAUTIFUL PEOPLE OF JAH,

DANCE TO THE RHYTHM OF THE DRUMS

AND CELEBRATE LIFE WITH ME, AND MY RETURN TO THE AFTER WORLD".

With that being said, the sound of Congo drums commenced playing a slow rhythmic beat. Mama Creo-lard's dark piercing eyes scoured the room like they were in search of prey. They haunted and intimidated everyone in the church; especially the likes of A.J.—who with an open bible covering his face sunk down deeper and deeper into his pew.

In a matter of seconds, the drummer started beating his bass drum so loud that everyone could feel it. The bass guitar player started plucking his bass so hard and loud that the windows in the church vibrated. And Sister Althea seemed to be possessed on the organ, screeching out sounds and notes so funky that they could've made the dead get up and dance. There was without a doubt a supernatural spirit in the church, because soon afterwards, a feeling of euphoria and bliss overcame everyone inside.

Hands were clapping, feet were tapping, and tambourines were wrapping. Great big women jumped up on the floor as if they had been reborn. They put their hands on their hip and danced in a circle from right to left; then they danced from left to right—including Miss Ella...

The spirit even hit deep inside the girls. Kim, Tamara, and Angie couldn't contain themselves any longer. They danced, shouted praises to the Lord and started speaking in tongues while dropping to the floor going into convulsions-- squirming around in the church aisles.

All of a sudden, Mama Creo-lard exerted a loud, frightful, supernatural squawking that sounded like an enormous bird. Then she stretched her arms out wide and brought her staff down to the floor and banged it three times. A powerful gust of wind blew through the church; the windows slammed shut, the doors locked up tight, and the sun light shining through the stain-glass windows of the church got brighter and brighter. And suddenly, the flickering of light from one window to the next created a kaleidoscope of beautiful colors inside the church.

Immediately following this hallowed experience, little children, and babies in their strollers began speaking in tongue. The Holy Water under the pulpit turned blue and bubbled out of its container, and all nine collection plates miraculously filled up with money.

Then, the sound of the Congo drums started beating faster, harder, and louder; it was as if they were in the deepest, darkest part of the African jungle. The drummer, the bass player, and the organist were mesmerized by the beat of the conga drums and their souls became a part of the music.

The choir was possessed by the unearthly spirit. They began swaying back and forth--around and about in circular motions. Even the sound of wild animals were present--giving the church an African safari like ambiance. Then the church members witnessed the seven-foot tall Jamaican Priestess do her bird dance, and as such, they fell under the spell of her hypnotic power and began dancing like they were in a Voodoo Ritual.

They danced, and they danced, and they danced with no recollection of time, or of what was happening to them. Then, several hours later, as sudden and miraculously as Mama Creo-lard appeared, she mysteriously disappeared. After that, there was complete silence in the church. The entire church congregation, with over 300 people in attendance, were still in a semi-hypnotic trance after Mama Creo-lard left. And not one of them could acknowledge or deny her presence in the church. But that didn't last long. Because A.J. inadvertently broke the silence when he slowly slid up from his seat with his bible wide-open covering his face.

And when he got the courage to bring the bible down completely from his face, he stood up and looked around the room, and a split second later, with no regard for where he was, he blurted out loud: "Whew! I'm Glad That Bitch Is Gone!"

Miss Ella abruptly turned around in her seat and frowned at him with a look of disgust on her face. She was too far away to slap the taste out of his mouth, but Earlene knew what to do; she was close enough to haul off and slap him upside his nappy ass head; and that's just what she did. And Leon was sitting right next to A.J, when she did it, and it just tore him to pieces; he couldn't stop laughing: "Ehee, hee-hee... Ehee-hee-hee..., Ehee, hee hee hee hee hee hee...!"

But the strangest thing happened after that. When the church members heard how silly his laughing sounded, it caught on like an infectious disease; his laughing had more than half the people in the church laughing.

As for The Reverend Kimble, when he came out of his zombie-like trance, he saw all the money piled up in the collection plates and had the ushers take it to his office to be counted and put in the church vault. And he was obviously thrilled beyond words--it was like a dream come true for him. But before they could count the money, he went to the podium and brazenly announced his last statement to the congregation: "Church Is Over, Go Home."

CHAPTER SEVEN

HOME COMING/AUNT ELLA'S HOUSE

After these half-starved kids piled on the bus, Miss Ella had Alvin stop at the closest KFC to get a two-piece chicken meal for everyone. Fortunately, it was a quick trip-- only a half mile down the road. And as quick as they got there to order their food; these kids devoured it even quicker.

Ten minutes later, Alvin pulled off the main road coming from town onto the freeway. After several minutes on the freeway, he pulled off at the Hopple Street exit and made a left turn at the intersection. After that, he drove a mile through the Mount Washington business district. Then he reached a side street and took a small stretch of road to the end of Colerain Ave and drove down a back alley where he pulled into an empty lot next to the house.

Some of the kids had never been there before--it was there first time being there. Nevertheless, it was dark and not easy to see how the house looked from the outside. But, it was a tall, spooky looking three-story row house. A few of the gray panels of siding were missing from the top portion of the house, but for the most part, on the inside, it was a spacious and comfortable place to live.

Anyway, as soon as Alvin parked the bus, everyone grabbed their belongings and pushed their way to the front of the bus. Although there were no lights on inside the house; outside in the yard there was just enough light for them to see the gate in the middle of the fence that surrounded the house.

It just so happened that the light that let them to see as much as they did see came from under the hood of a car on the side of the house. Uncle Riley— Aunt Ella's Husband was still under the hood working on it; he had been there sense early that morning and he was determined to get it running. He was obviously frustrated because he was mumbling and fidgeting with his tools, trying to find the right size tool to fit a part he was going to replace.

Anyway, as soon as they got off the bus, they heard barking and scuffling feet back and forth. It was Rah-Mel, a full- grown German Shepherd. He was Uncle Riley's pride and joy. Rah-Mel's ferocious bark sent chills up and down their backs. Lucky for them he was inside a five by ten-foot caged fence inside the confines of the fence in the backyard.

Anyway, Rah-Mel could smell the food they'd been eating when they passed by his cage and it sent him into a wild frenzy. He started barking, running back and forth, trying to climb the fence inside his cage. And as such, being scared out of their wits, these kids cautiously passed by his cage and ran up the porch steps--pushing their way inside the backdoor.

Miss Ella was the exception to the rule though. She didn't take any mess off of him, or the last two mutts Riley brought home. If she got tired of hearing him barking, she'd stare him dead in his eyes with a look that could make the second-hand on a clock stop. Then she'd tell him to Shut up and Go Sit down! It worked every time. Rah-Mel would walk away with his tale between his legs and lay down in his cage.

Meanwhile, lurking in the darkness, Alvin and A J. were the last ones to leave the bus. Alvin had good reason to be last. He didn't want to be noticed by his daddy. He knew that if he saw him, he was going to ask him for help fixing that car, and Alvin had no intentions of getting dirty and greasy and being up all night.

However, Miss Ella had already stopped to give Riley a chicken dinner on the way to the house, and through their exchange of information, he knew that Alvin was somewhere close by. And sure enough, the next sound Alvin heard was his daddy's voice saying: "hey boy, come here and help me put this engine in this car." And, it was obvious that Alvin was pissed! He was tired, sleepy, and hungry just like everybody else. Anyone listening could tell that he was overflowing with disgust because he began mumbling to himself: "God-dam, daddy! I don't feel like fooling with that raggedy-ass car tonight! Shit! Hell Naw!" His daddy didn't hear him, but A. J.'s ears were wide open, and he knew just how upset his dad was, but that didn't stop him from snickering. Then he saw his dad walk away and disappear down the alley. However, knowing that his grandfather would never ask him for help, A. J. offered to help him anyway; not really meaning it, but he told him: "I'll help you, Grandpa."

THE NEXT MORNING

The next morning Miss. Ella was up early preparing breakfast for the kids. She was in the kitchen stirring a huge pot of oatmeal, and the only early risers to assist her were Lavada and Danielle. They sat up the kitchen table with the necessary amount of bowls, cups and spoons.

Lavada and Danielle both had a sweet tooth just like Miss Ella, so she let them get away with eating all kinds of snacks before dinner--cakes, candy, cookies or whatever they wanted to eat hold them over until dinner time."

Nevertheless, when the oatmeal was done, they sat down at the table to eat before the others made their random decent to the kitchen.

The first one down the steps was Samantha. It took her a while, but that ten-year-old, feisty filly made it down that long, narrow flight of steps from the third floor with no problem.

She and some of the other girls were up late last night talking, having a good time, and getting to know each other. They talked and talked, and talked and they realized that they all had a lot in common.

For instance, all of them had the tenacity to hold on to their money so tight that the eagle on a dollar bill would screamed. And they all had similar methods of operation, and that included blackmail, extortion, and snitching. And although they appeared to be shy, sweet and gentle girls; they could also be as mean as a rattlesnake.

The next two occupants to appear were Kim and Tamara. They were the oldest females of the bunch. They were also up late last night recalling old friends and old times. They were bright, intelligent girls with gifted voices, and they loved listening and singing gospel songs and preaching the word. But, if you pushed them too far, they'd "Tap Dance on Some Ass."

Whistling, He-hawing, and humming their way down the steps next was Alvin Junior and Walter Junior; (AKA) A. J. and Chunky, respectively. They had a long night of reminiscing, fun, and laughter. They talked about things in the past and played video games until they fell asleep. They were like brothers growing up. For A.J., it was like losing his best friend when his Aunt Wanda packed them up and moved to Atlanta. Nevertheless, A.J. still got to see Chunk every other summer. They were two care-free, happy-go-lucky kids in pursuit of happiness, and that included each, every, and any kind of prank imaginable.

Squeaking down the stair steps next, in their size 15 shoes, was Big Lee and David Alafia, (AKA) D.A. Their dads are brothers, and as such, they had a close bond. They are very athletically endowed and they love sports; mainly football and basketball, and on any given day they'd hustle money playing basketball or betting on football games.

The next two to the breakfast table were Earlene and Angie. Last night they got to know each other all over again. They talked about everything from boys and school, to life in general. Earlene always had Angie's back if anything went wrong with her. And Angie had her back. She'd be there to calm Earlene down when she got upset, or if she did something to get in herself trouble.

Bringing up the rear, were two legends in their own mind, Ernie and Monty. They eased on down the stairs to the breakfast table rapping to some made up lyrics. Besides that, they thought they were some players. Ernie thought he was a Mack and Monty was his protege. Basically, they were just two aspiring rap amateurs with delusions of grandeur.

The last loafers down the steps were, Little Gary-AKA(Popsicle) Little Leon, and Leroy. Other than being the undisputed products of their environment, there are several descriptions that fit them. Popsicle could be described as a rambling, scamming, gambling, money snatcher. He packed a 9-inch switchblade in his shoe, and his extracurricular activities included: purse snatching, car- jacking, rolling winos in alleys, and if he could, he'd steal the funk off a pile of dog shit.

Leroy was just as scandalous. He was a pistol-packing bad-ass, and he was in the developmental stage of being a big-time dope-dealing-dumbass. His mom was desperate to get him away from the dope-slinging hustle in the streets where they lived, the elements of danger that living in that kind of environment couldn't bring anything but heartaches and misery.

Little Leon was another story, He loved getting high, and he did it at every turn-- morning, noon, and especially at night. He was constantly laughing like a hyena, day-in, and day-out. And from the sound of his laughter, anyone with good sense would think that he was either high as a kite or nut case.

Anyway, these three were last to strut to the kitchen to eat breakfast. But, before they could sit down at the table, the 'Head Negros in Charge.' Kim and Tamara told them to go wash your face and hands before you sit down at the table. Well, their reaction to their command was thought of as being too obtrusive in the minds of these incredulous creeps, and as such, their reactions were followed by moans and groans of resentment being mumbled under their breath.

CHAPTER EIGHT

THE OATMEAL WAR

Nonetheless, when the three bad seeds returned from the wash room, everyone was sitting at the table to eating. Miss Ella and the other girls had eaten earlier, and now they were in the basement washing clothes. Furthermore, in addition to helping Miss Ella wash clothes, they were filling up cups of Kool-Aid to put in the deep freezer to make ice-balls. Therefore, during this time span, A.J. found the perfect opportunity to tell everybody a new joke. It was the story about:

THE DOG THAT COULD WALK ON WATER

"Two old men ran into each other at a lake one day with nothing to do but enjoy the peace and quiet. One man brought his dog, Fido with him to keep him company. They sat down and spoke to each other, and then, the man with the dog started bragging on his dog, and he told the other man that his dog could do an amazing trick. So, the other man said: "O' Yeah! What can he do?" He said watch this. He picked up a stick and threw it a little-ways out in the water and told Fido to fetch. The dog walked out on the water, picked the stick up, brought it back and laid it down next to his master's feet.

He looked at the man and asked him, "Did you notice anything unusual about my dog?" And the man said: "No, I didn't notice anything unusual about your dog." So, he did it again. He threw the stick in the water a little further this time and told Fido to fetch. So, Fido walked out on the water again, picked the stick up, and brought it back to his master. He turned to look at the man again and said: "Did you notice anything unusual about my dog this time"? And the man said No again.

So, by now the man was getting frustrated and he told him to watch closely. This time he threw the stick halfway across the lake and he told Fido to fetch. Fido ran out across the lake and picked the stick up, then he ran right back with it and gave it to his master. The man looked at him again and said: "Did you notice anything unusual about my dog this time"! The man looked at him and said: "Yeah, Man! That damn dog can't swim"! "Ah ha-ha-ha-ha-ha-ha-ha! Ah, Ha ha ha ha ha ha ha ha ha! You get it! That damn dog can't swim!"

As expected, Leon busted a gut laughing at the joke. But, disgusted by both the joke and A.J. was Earlene, and what she did next proved just how much she disliked his joke. Furthermore, it was her flagrant reaction to the joke that caused the catalyst that sparked a chain reaction of unbelievable chaos.

First of all, Leon couldn't stop laughing and he started choking off the oatmeal he was swallowing at the time. However, no-one else at the table seemed to care or give A.J. the time of day. That is until Earlene flung a tablespoon of oatmeal between his eyes and called him a moron. Well, Leon saw that too, and he laughed even louder, and this time, everybody did. But, with a big wad of oatmeal sliding down his nose and dripping from his upper lip--A.J. Retaliated. He slung a wad of oatmeal right back at her, but he missed. Earlene ducked and instead of hitting her, it hit Angie upside her head and knocked her glasses halfway off her face.

"Oh no you didn't negro," She shouted indignantly. Then she immediately flung a huge load of oatmeal right back at him, but her aim was off too, and she wound up plastering Chunk dead in his mouth. "Dang Angie! He garbled with a load of oatmeal stuck in his mouth. Why'd you hit me?" "Oh, I'm sorry, Chunk, I was trying to hit that fool next to you, but my spoon slipped."

After that, the big sisters, Kim and Tamara got a piece of the action. They were sick and tired of hearing Leon laughing like a nut, and they were tired of hearing Popsicle trying to go for bad selling wolf-tickets. He kept on saying "I bet nobody better not hit me with that shit!" So, they decided to shut both of them up.

Well, these two were thinking the same thought. Because they both glanced over and saw a twenty-pound bag of rock salt sitting next to the kitchen door-- half opened and easy to get to. So, a devilish thought more or less popped into the minds of these two otherwise angles. They looked at the salt and looked at each other and started grinning like a cat that just swallowed a canary.

Both of them grabbed a hand full of rock salt and mixed it in with the oatmeal in their bowls. Kim mixed hers up to the size of a baseball and was the first one to stand up and rifle it from across the room like a major league pitcher. She hit Popsicle right upside his head and he went down like a wounded soldier.

Tamara fired away next; her aim was just as good, but instead of hitting Leon in his mouth, she hit him dead in his throat. Not only did she stop him from laughing, but the impact from the blow cut off his breathing.

When A.J. saw what happened he busted his gut laughing. And when Angie saw it, she wasn't laughing at all, she was still sitting at the table wiping oatmeal from her hair and cleaning her glasses—and of course, she was still mad as hell. So, she just sat there in silence and watched her stupid cousin, A.J. and the rest of the wild bunch act like fools.

Well, when Popsicle got up off the floor, he was trying to find out what happened to him. So, he shouted: "Who hit me, God-dammit!" And Kim spoke up quick, loud, and proud and said: "I did fool, what you going to do about it?" Well, he started walking towards her like Mr. Get-Bad, and like he was going to do something to her. But as soon as he got close enough to see her holding that cast-iron skillet behind her back, he quickly slowed his roll; he turned around, walked back and sat down, and he shut the fuck up. Well, A.J. was tickled to death when he saw that happen, so he tried to rally Popsicle into standing his ground: He told him: "Go ahead, man—show her what ya working with, Popsicle! She's a heavy weight, but don't let that scare you. You can handle her-- do her like Ike did Tina...!"

Anyway, Angie was still sitting across the table from A.J., and by now, she had wiped all the oatmeal from her hair and cleaned up her glasses. And, she didn't want to have anything more to do with the oatmeal fight. And as such, she kept her eye on everything going on around her, and she watched while everybody had their own private oatmeal war.

However, while still sitting across the table from, A.J.--he got even sillier. Angie had just happened to put her glasses back on, and A.J saw how thick the lens in them was, he just had to say something dumb to infuriate her. He said: "Damn Angie, your glasses are so thick that I bet when you look at a road map you can see people driving in their cars smiling and waving back at you and shit!"

And that was just enough for her to hear to do what she did next. Even Earlene couldn't believe what this soft-spoken, highly patient little girl did; but it happened. Angie turned into a fireball. She exploded across that table like she had been shot out of a cannon and knocked A.J. out of his chair.

Then she got on top of him and grabbed him by his head and banged it on the floor. The surprise from the attack had him in shock, but after a good seven or eight good bangs of his head against the floor, they pulled her off of him.

Well, Miss Ella was still in the basement when she heard the banging against the floor, and she was wondering what in the hell is going on upstairs. So, she ran up the steps, opened the door and saw everybody standing around in a circle looking down at the floor. A.J. was laying on the floor on his back with his eyes rolled back in his head. But, when Miss Ella broke through the circle of spectators, she saw A.J. laying on the floor--lifeless and halfway unconscious. Then she looked up and around at all the innocent faces around her and said: "Um Hum, whose gonna tell me who kicked his ass this time?"

CHAPTER NINE

THE HOG CALLING

Over the next few days, they found out a lot about Miss Ella's ways--she never gave up on trying to discipline them. And immediately following their outrageous oatmeal war, she put together a cleaning crew and assigned them specific work duties. They included washing the walls, mopping the floor, washing the dishes, and cleaning oatmeal off the furniture.

After their tedious work excursion ended, Miss Ella was able to get her irreversible point across to them in a few words. What it all boiled down to was letting them know who the head negro in charge was, and that "They Couldn't Shit the Shitter." And as such, she held them responsible for respecting each other, and her house,

On a different note, Samantha was a long way from being happy. She was getting home sick. She was waiting for her Grandma to call like she had promised, but she hadn't heard anything from her yet. Especially when (super players) Ernie and Monty kept hogging the phone. They had it tied up most of the day; her grandma may have called and not been able to get through she thought. But she always kept her ears open to hear the phone ring just in case.

Other than that, while everyone else ran around the house like chickens in a barnyard, she made Rah-Mel her new friend. Every morning after breakfast she'd take her left over table scraps out back and feed them to him. And as unbelievable as it seemed, sometimes she'd sit down next to his cage and read to him out of her story book. Nobody had ever seen anyone calm Rah-Mel down the way she did. It was highly unusual; however, the two of them could communicate like bosom buddies.

Furthermore, Uncle Riley had gotten to the point of developing a rapport with Samantha. It was obviously due to the affect she had on Rah-Mel. It tickled him to pieces to see the way they got along. Therefore, he let her get away with just about anything.

The other knuckleheads in the house were a different story. They were a bunch of contemptible assholes as far as he was concerned. He found that out after he almost broke his leg slipping on a pile of oatmeal on the kitchen floor that they missed when they were cleaning up. The wiseasses applauded when he slipped and did the splits like he was James Brown. But he never lost his cool, and he rarely, if ever got upset, yelled, or shouted at any of them.

Anyway, after a full two weeks of the kids living in his house, Uncle Riley still paid them little to no attention at all, He rarely notice them because most of the time he was up early in the morning underneath the hood of one of his cars. And on this particular day, his hard work paid off. It was the weekend before the 4th of July holiday, and he needed a good car up and running. The car he was working on wasn't bran new, and it wasn't an ugly piece of junk. It was a station wagon that had rarely used, and it had good tires on it.

Well, a long ride was ahead of them now. This was an important trip that came about due to Uncle Riley having a buddy living in the country that raised hogs on his farm. Every year at this time, Uncle Riley and Miss Ella were welcome to come out to get a hog or two slaughtered and dressed. Therefore, he needed the station wagon that he had just fixed because it gave him plenty of room to bring his haul back home in one trip.

Anyway, it rained all night long and well into the afternoon that day. Uncle Riley and Alvin were up at 6:00 that morning and were ready to go at 7:00. Furthermore, some of the kids were up as well and they wanted to ride with them. So, they all piled in the station wagon, not knowing the extent of the drive, yet relieved to get out the house for a while. A road filled with fog was in front of them and a dark sky was above them.

The Johnson farm was in the next county on the outskirts of Hamilton, OH. It took about an hour to drive along the long, winding country roads next to the Great Miami River. Nevertheless, they packed themselves in the car like sardines in a can; AJ., D.A., Chunk, Popsicle, and Leon had to struggle to get in the back seat of the car. Furthermore, they had no idea that it was going to take as long as it took to get where they were going. Samantha was in the car too. She was the only girl, but she was wide awake, and she proved that she was as sharp as a tack by using her wily wit to talk Uncle Riley out of the window seat; he rode shotgun while Alvin did the driving.

Miss Ella was up also, and she was waiting on the rest of the girls to get up. She intended of having her baby brother, Joel drive the church bus to bring her and the rest of the girls out later that morning. Just as in the past, she was welcomed to pick a slew of vegetables from the farmer's garden, and she needed the girl's help.

Anyway, the rain was still drizzling and the dark clouds were still hovering above them during their drive there until the time they arrived. And as soon as they arrived, Alvin and his daddy got out of the car and carefully made their way around the puddles of water in the dirt rode, and walked up the muddy driveway to the farmer's door.

When they reached the door, old man Johnson was right there to open it as soon as they stepped on the porch. He came out the door and spoke to them in a loud, enthusiastic voice: "Hey Riley, How Yall Doing? Yall Ready To Kill These Hogs"? Uncle Riley looked up at the six-foot four-inch farmer and said: "Hell yeah, Johnson," and he said, "Well, come on, follow me."

A.J. had gotten out of the car and was standing behind a tree relieving his bladder from the long ride up there when he saw his dad and his Grandfather walking toward the rear of the house. So, he told everyone in the car to get out so they could follow them. And as such, they all got out the car and followed them around back and down a grassy slope to a large pig pen. Inside it were two humongous hogs. Their names were Daisy and Lucifer; they were standing in the middle of the pen--covered with mud and oblivious to what was about to happen to them.

There was no way to prepare these kids for what was about to happen next—especially Samantha. Therefore, the anxious farmer wasted no time at all. As soon as he opened the gate and hollered Suey! .... Suey! .... Suey! ...., the hogs came running toward him. Daisy, was the smaller hog that got there first, and no sooner than he threw a handful of grain on the ground in front her, she buried her shout in it and greedily devoured it from the mud.

Seconds later, the farmer aimed his rifle at the top of that hog's head and shot it. The hog fell over dead. It was a gruesome sight, and a particularly troublesome sight for a ten-year-old girl to see. When Samantha heard the gunfire, she cringed and watched the hog drop to the ground. Then she grabbed a hold of Uncle Riley and buried her face in his jacket.

The rest of the boys were awe struck. The sight of the blood coming from the hole in that hog's head was sickening to them. Some of them couldn't stomach the sight and threw up right there on the spot. But, it wasn't over yet, the count was one down and one to go.

Nevertheless, the farmer's sons, Jake and Jerome were there to tie ropes to the hog's feet and drag it up the slope to the barn. By this time, Lucifer had retreated to the far side of the pen—snorting and shaking his head back and forth like a rebellious bull. If you could have read his mind you would have thought he was saying, (You're Not going to Get Me That Easy). He was every bit of 100 pounds heavier than Daisy and meaner than Black Rhino.

However, the timing of Lucifer's execution was delayed. Lucky for him, but unfortunate for Uncle Riley. The farmer had used his last rifle shell when he shot Daisy, and neither the farmer nor his sons could make the drive to the city right then. Furthermore, it was about an hour-long drive to the closest ammo store in town. So, as it turned out, the farmer's wife was the only one capable of making the drive.

Meanwhile, back at the barn, Jake and Jerome, were in the process of tying the hog to a meat hook and raising it on a pulley hanging from the rafter in the barn. Off to the side sat a fifty-gallon barrel of scalding hot water being heated underneath a blazing fire.

Once inside the barn, everyone gathered around to see the next gruesome sight. Samantha and her fearless five cousins where about to see something that would make a lasting impression in their minds. They had never seen anything like this before and it was too late to back out now.

Well, when they saw it, they thought they were watching a scene from a horror movie. The farmer walked up to the hog hanging in the air, and with his hunting knife in his hand he raised it to the top of the hog's belly and slit it wide open--right down the middle. After that, all they saw was blood, guts, and gore falling out piling up on the ground in front of them. Samantha gasped and covered her face with her hands. The reaction to the sight overwhelmed her to the point of tears and she ran to the car and locked the doors. She refused to talk to anyone for the rest of the day.

On the flip side, the boys blurted out all kinds of exclamatory remarks when they saw the disgusting sight. On top of that, they tried to refrain from throwing up what little they had left in their stomachs. And as such, they ran out of the barn to get away from the sight of it. The farmer's sons were sure enough getting a big kick out of their reaction; they laughed, taunted, and teased them for having weak stomachs. Anyway, they lowered the hog down into the barrel of scalding hot water to remove the hair from its hide, and after that, they skinned it and to cut it into different parts.

Soon afterwards, Miss Ella and the rest of the girls showed up. Ernie, Monty, Lee and Leroy were nowhere to be found when they were leaving, everyone else was there. Miss Ella coaxed her brother, Joel into driving for them out, and all he got in return was a reminder of the harsh reality of living in the country.

Anyway, with all of that over and done, Uncle Riley was getting restless. He wanted that other hog, and he wanted it now. The farmer's wife hadn't returned yet with the shells and he was ready do just about anything to kill that hog. So, as the minutes passed by, one of the farmer's sons mentioned using a sledgehammer to knock the hog unconscious and then cutting its throat so it would bleed to death. Well, it didn't take long for Uncle Riley to go along with that idea. And sure enough, with the farmer's approval, that's exactly what they set out to do.

Well, it eventually stopped raining and the sun was positioned high in the sky; it was getting hot and humid. Miss Ella and the girls were there right on time to pick whatever, and as much she wanted from the farmer's garden. However, as soon as the girls stepped off the bus, the smell coming from the barn got to them--it was awful. It was too much for them to handle. And accordingly, due to the disgusting smell, a permanent frown was etched on their faces. However, it didn't last for long. The smell wasn't as bad from where they were picking vegetables, and they were all able to do their part in the garden regardless of the mud they had to trudge through. However, the real excitement was just beginning down at the pig pen.

So, with no more thought about the matter, the mission began. The lineup went as such. Uncle Riley was first on deck to wield a 20-pound sledgehammer at Lucifer. However, he didn't know about, Lucifer. Lucifer wasn't the typical type of hog. He was more of a wild boar, and he had a heightened sense for survival. He wasn't about to go down without a fight, and that's a fact they all soon came to realize.

Anyway, Uncle Riley picked up that 20-pound sledgehammer and went head hunting. But in his eagerness to kill that hog he made a foolish mistake before anyone could stop him. He went to the far end of the fence and stood on the top rail, and when he saw Lucifer came close enough he tried to knock his brains out. Well, Lucifer eventually came close enough for him take a swing. But after he swung, something remarkable happened, he missed hitting Lucifer and did a head over heels summersault and landed face first in a pile of hog shit. Well, if he had been on the Olympic swim team the judges would have probably voted to give him a perfect score of all tens.

Everybody thought that hog had eyes in the back of his head. Lucifer scampered away just as Uncle Riley was about to hit him. The only logical reason they could figure was because of the sun casting a shadow when he stood on that fence directly behind him.

Anyway, it was a Kodak camera moment that made everybody laugh. And accordingly, from that moment on, Uncle Riley had to learn how to live with the new name the farmer gave him, "Old Shit Face."

The next slugger on deck was Alvin. He helped his daddy up; got him out of the mud, and out of the pig pen, and then he got in the pen and squared off with Lucifer. The other boys were spread out all around the outside of the pen. A.J. and Chunk were at one end; Popsicle, D.A., and Leon were at the other end, and the farmer's sons, Jake and Jerome were on opposite sides of the pen.

Then they all started shouting and banging on the rails to distract the hog and get its attention so Alvin could get a chance to surprised attack it. That's when Lucifer began squealing, and snorting, and shaking his head back and forth. And as they got louder-- the madder that hog got. But Lucifer never took his eyes off Alvin—he stood there in the middle of that muddy pen staring him down.

All of a sudden Lucifer took off running. He headed toward Alvin like he was a practice dummy on a football field, but Alvin didn't back down. He stood his ground like a fearless hero.

So, when the hog got close enough, he took a superhero swing at him, and just like his daddy, he missed. Likewise, the weight of that sledgehammer and the force behind his swing spent him around so fast and so far, that it was impossible for him to stop. He wound up with his back to the hog, and before he knew it, Lucifer had his snout halfway up Alvin's ass. He was pent against the fence hollering: "Somebody Get This Motherfucker Off Of Me!"

But, to everyone's surprise, A.J. jumped in the pen to help his dad. Alvin was at the other end of the pen trying to stop Lucifer from ramming him in his ass, and A.J. was running to his rescue. But suddenly, Lucifer backed up off Alvin, and turned around and spotted A.J. running toward him.

Well, right at that moment A. J's bravery fell short. He saw Lucifer back up off his dad, so he tried his best to stop and change directions; but the manure laden mud didn't make it easy, and he slipped, slid, and holler like a bitch when he saw Lucifer coming towards him.

In a matter of seconds Lucifer had his snout buried between A.J.'s hind legs, and he picked him up and tossed him in the air like he was a rag doll. By the time A.J. fell back down to earth, Little Walter and Popsicle were inside the pen dragging his muddy, mangled body toward the fence.

That hog was incredible. He was a monster. It was just like the farmer said-- He's a mean sum-bitch. That hog fought them like a warrior. Walter was on one side of A.J. swinging a tree branch at the hog every time it came near, and Popsicle was on his other side with his switchblade opened and swinging it at him like he was in a gang fight.

While all of this was going on, Leon and D.A. were behind the fence smoking a blunt, but they did put their supervisory skills to work. He and D.A. were shouting out instructions to the both of them, and at the same time they were sucking and puffin on a joint. "That's right, pull him over here, I got him. Hurry up! Ut Oh! Here he comes again. Hit him in the head, Walter—show that big ole rascal how Yall do it in the ATL. Popsicle, watch out—you better cut him next time. Here he comes again, Pop. Cut him, quick now, Popsicle. Awe, shit, you missed again. Ehee- hee-hee...Ehee- hee-hee-hee. …. That's all right. Try it again!"

Then Leon took a toke from the joint and nonchalantly said: "Yall gonna feel a lot better after yall smoke some of this 'Scrilla': Ehee, hee-hee..."

Interestingly enough, Joel wasn't far off. He was observing the (Massacre at The Comedy Corral) from the barn. But he eventually walked down to the pen to see what all the drama was about. And well, Joel being Joel; he wound up smoking that blunt with them and giving his expert supervisory advice.

Well, right after Walter and Popsicle pulled A.J. to safety, A.J. was on the other side of the fence now—fussing, cussing, and selling wolf-tickets to the hog.

However, soon after that, the farmer's wife showed up. They heard her yelling down to the farmer that she had made it back with the rifle shells. And as soon as he got them, he told Jake and Jerome to stop laughing and get the ropes so they could do their job the way they were taught.

They looked like two rodeo cowboys. They both threw a lasso around Lucifer's head from opposite sides of the pen and tied the end of their ropes to the side of the fence so he couldn't move one way or the other. Then, old man Johnson opened the gate and walked up to that hog. He took aim and shot him in the head two times.

But, Uncle Riley was still furious about what that hog did to him. So, after the farmer shot him, he snatched the rifle out of his hands; took aim at that hog and shot him in the head four more times. Then he spit on it and said: "You Rotten Motherfucker!"

After that, Jake, Jerome and the farmer stared at Riley for a long time with a look on their faces that said: (That Nigga's Crazy).

CHAPTER TEN

THE COWMAN COM-ETH

It was half past noon and the sun was radiating beams of heat that not only dried the ground, it also dried the mud-mixed manure on A.J.'s clothes. So, Leon spoke his mind and let him know flat out that: "A.J. You Smell Like Shit,"

A.J. could have went the rest of the day without hearing that remark, but when he heard it, it pissed him off. And it started a long argument that ended with the obvious fact that he had just been assaulted by a hog. But, it still didn't change the fact that he did smell like shit, and that he needed to put some water on that shit.

Anyway, after A.J. calmed down, he saw his dad and Grandfather on the side of the farmer's house using the water hose to wash up. But, instead of waiting for them to finish, he saw Jake and Jerome coming from the barn and asked them if there was another place where he could wash up.

Well, Jake and Jerome stopped what they were doing and looked at each other with a conniving grin on their faces. Then Jake turned and said: "Yeah, there's a creek down that hill over there where you can wash up, but you better watch out for the cowman." A split-second later Jerome said: "Yeah, you can wash off down there but if the cowman catches you He'll Fuck You Dry!" Then they started laughing like two psychopaths.

Well, A.J. And the other boys heard what they said, but, in a way they didn't hear them, and with A.J. being the type of know-it-all leader he was, he said: "Man, Forget those Fools. Those Hillbillies are just trying to scare us." So, instead of taking them seriously, they played follow the leader behind A.J and found a way down the hill.

They came to a cliff where there was at least a thirty-foot drop-off and saw a stream of water at the bottom that ran into a larger body of water. But it wasn't like they thought it would be. It was larger than they thought it would be--from one end to as far as they could see.

Anyway, they stopped for a minute to search for a way to get to the bottom, and sure enough, about twenty feet to the left they saw an entrance to a trail that led them down the hill. They followed the trail down to the bottom of the hill and saw a small body of water in front of them. And they also found themselves surrounded by giant trees and all sorts of wildlife.

So, funkier than fearful of the wildlife, A.J., Chunk, and Popsicle waded in a shallow section of the water and rinsed off their clothes and their bodies.

While they were doing that, D.A. And Leon had a rock skipping contest. And as such, D.A. boasted that he was the best with nine consecutive skips. So, as soon as the other boys were through rinsing off they joined in on the contest. And naturally, the contest resulted in all five of them proclaiming to be the victor of the contest.

After that, Chunk was the first one to spot a couple of tire-swings half-way up the hill hanging from a rope in the trees. And no sooner than he saw it, he made his way up that hill to get one of them. He slid into one of the swings and belted out a loud Mississippi River-rat yell while he was swinging out over the middle of that water. Then he slipped out of the tire and plunged into the water like a Navy rescue diver.

Furthermore, fifty or so yards away from where they were, there was a boardwalk. It was barely noticeable, but it was sticking out from the bank. In addition to that, he noticed that there was a home-made raft with three large tire-inner-tubes sitting on top of it.

Anyway, Chunk's act of reckless fun appealed to D.A. so much that he grabbed the other tire-swing and took it for a ride over the water. And, by shear accident, his foot made contact with the side of A.J.'s shoulder when he swung by him. It knocked him off balance just enough for him to bump into Popsicle. But, it didn't stop there; it created a domino effect that resulted in Popsicle losing his balance; he bumped into Leon and all three of them wound up in the water.

Leon was so high that he got paranoid when he fell in the water. He hollered like a schoolgirl when he fell in and started splashing around in the water shouting: "Help! I can't swim, I can't swim. Awe.... shit, I'm gonna drown, I'm gonna drown!"

But, Popsicle and A.J. were in the water right next to him when he fell in, and when they felt their feet touch the bottom of the lake they stood up, and told him to stand up, and when his feet touched the bottom of the lake he felt like a fool.

Anyway, after a while the cool water had neutralized their hot bodies, and that's when they started having fun. Chunk and D.A were up for the downstroke-- they had a swimming race. All of them had their clothes off down to their draws--just splashing and thrashing around in the water. Then Chunk and D.A. swam down to the raft an untied it from the boardwalk, and before long, they were standing on top of it navigating their way back toward the other boys. When they reached them, they tossed them a tire inner-tube. And that's when they got the courage to venture further down that eerie looking stream to explore the unknown territory.

So, foot pedaling on inner-tubes, and pole-pushing a homemade raft, they took off down the stream. They got a good quarter mile downstream with no end in sight and everything was fine so far. They traveled through a narrow corridor with towering mud and clay banked cliffs on one side, and a largely populated brush-filled body of land and trees was on the other side. Everything seemed to be serene, undisturbed, and mysterious.

But, as they traveled a little further downstream they saw a lot of dead fish floating in the water, and the further downstream they went, the more dead fish they saw—laying on the bank rotting with the middle eaten out of them.

After traveling few yards further, they noticed strange looking footprints in the sand on the bank, and all of a sudden, Chunk saw something moving in the brush along the shore. He couldn't really make out what it was, but he noticed that it was moving in their direction. He told D.A., and D.A. told the rest of the boys, but they didn't see anything either.

Right after that, things got spooky. The water started flowing faster and they kept moving downstream faster. It felt like they were headed for a waterfall up ahead and that's when they immediately decided to turn back.

However, right after their decision to turn back, there was a tremendous cloud burst. The sky turned black, and raindrops the size of marbles poured down on them and pounded the water. Then a strong, violent wind came from the opposite direction and slowed down their effort to get back. That's when they panicked, and that led to them pedal on those inner-tubes and pushing that raft harder and faster.

Eventually they started moving again at a strong, steady pace, but then they heard the sound of leaves rustling and tree branches cracking in the brush. D.A. and Chunk kept looking back to see what was causing the noise, but it was hard to see anything through the drenching rain and the thick brush along the shore.

Then the saw something--it was a frightening sight. D.A. and Chunk saw a hairy, nasty looking man-like creature standing on the shore, Well, their first thought was that it was a Big Foot. Its body was half-way hidden in the brush as it stood there on the bank; it was glaring at them with blood red eyes—growling and grumbling like a crazed beast.

All of a sudden they yelled: "Bigfoot! It's a Bigfoot following us Yall! Yall its a Bigfoot following us!" Right after that, they heard thunder rumbling, and immediately following that, they heard a sound they'd never heard before. It sounded like a sick cow mooing in pain, but it was a hundred times louder than a normal cow's mooing, and it went on and on.

But, after the sound stopped, they all saw it. It looked like a creature from hell-- unbelievably grotesque, and this time when they saw it, it rose up on two hind legs and bolstered out another loud, painful sounding cry that made their assholes pucker and piss run down their leg.

But during that brief time span, it was still hard to see; however, A.J. made an acute observation. He said: "Hey Chunk., how many legs does a Bigfoot have"? Chunk said two. Then A.J. took another long, hard look at that creature and said: "That Mutha-fucka got Four Legs! That ain't no Goddamn Bigfoot!" "Let's Get The Fuck Out Of Here"!

The first thought that crossed A.J.'s mind was that (now I know what those two country fucks were laughing about).

D.A. And Chunk immediately jumped off the raft into the water, and all of them took off swimming like a swarm of dolphins. And, when they took off, so did that creature—in a gallop along the shore—it was keeping up with their every stroke they made.

Then it let out another long, horrendous, painful sounding cry that was so loud it vibrated the walls in that canyon-- mud, clay, and rocks started falling off in huge chunks-- so large that they made ripples in the water that overflowed the bank. But miraculously, as soon as they made it back to where they started, the rain stopped. And as quick as they got there, they were even quicker about grabbing their clothes and running up that hill-- slipping and sliding their way to the top.

The terror-stricken look on their faces said it all. They had all saw what they saw, but somehow none of them could find the right words to describe what they saw. And with dilated eyes and jaw-dropping mouths; that same look of shock stayed on their faces the rest of the way home.

But the final straw was seeing those two crazy ass farm boys before they pulled off. Jake and Jerome showed up just in time to say good-bye. And when these boys heard their voices from the back seat of the car, they turned around to see them waving good-bye to them with sadistic grins on their faces.

CHAPTER ELEVEN

FUNK HITS THE FAN/ SEXUAL HEALING

They got home right as the bright orange sun was sinking down to the horizon, and as such, everyone was tired from the drive and glad to be home. They got off the bus and out of the car and immediately began taking the fruits of their labor to the house. But, instead of A.J. helping unload the packages of meat from the station wagon and taking them to the basement door with the other boys, he went straight to his Grandma and helped her off the bus.

Then he walked with her to the back door--helping her by carrying a bag of collard greens and a bag of potatoes. When they got inside, he sat the bags on the kitchen table and turned on the kitchen light. But, as he turned around to head back out the door, he heard strange noises in the front room. Through the sound of what should have been silence, he heard the distinctive sound of moans and groans, and laughter, and he smelled a very familiar smell.

When he stopped to listen more intently, he suddenly remembered that the other boys were still at home. Likewise, Miss Ella stopped what she was doing when she heard the noises and froze like a statue in the middle of the kitchen floor. Furthermore, her was nose in the air sniffing it like a radar detector. She was trying to figure out where she smelled that funky smell before too. And ultimately, her sixth sense quickly concluded that something devilish was going on in her house.

But, before she could set out to get to the bottom of it, A. J. had already busted a move to the front room to deliver a message. He knew that the moaning and groaning sounds he heard weren't coming from the television, and he definitely knew what pussy smelled like. So, when he got to the front room, he looked inside and saw just what he expected to see. Ernie and Monty were in there getting it on with two super-freaks. They were all half naked—Kissing, humping and grinding; moaning and groaning.

There were empty wine cooler bottles and beer cans everywhere; on the table and floor; half smoked blunts where in the ashtray; a deck of cards lay open and half scattered all over the table; pretzels and potato chips were all over the floor.

Anyway, he whispered to them, "Hey, you damn fools, Grandma is in the other room. You better get them the hell out of here!" But, by the time he finished warning them, he looked up and saw his Grandma standing in behind him. She gave him a scornful look, and after he tried to block her from going into the living room she gave him a stern command to "Move out the way!"

When she looked inside, and she couldn't believe her eyes. Visions of Sodom and Gomorrah suddenly flashed through her mind--she had a conniption. She screamed and cried out: "Oh lord help me Jesus! Help me Jesus! Oh God just take me, take me, God! Right Now! Right Now, take me lord! take me now...!"

Then, she got so light headed that she fainted, and all three-hundred pounds of her robust body fell on A.J. He was so shocked when she fell that he screamed for help at the top of his lungs. He desperately tried to hold her up the best he could, but she was too much woman for his weak little arms to handle, and it seemed like hours to him, but luckily some of the girls came running to his rescue and helped him set her down in a chair.

Shocked at what was happening, Ernie and Monty jumped up and rushed to put their clothes on before she regained consciousness. Then they rushed to clean up the living room before the funk hit the fan.

Well, by the time the two girls had gotten dressed; in their hast to get out the front door, Kim recognized one of the girls. "Peaches, she said, is that you?" Peaches turned away with a sheepish look on her face and didn't answer, but Kim walked up to her to get a closer look, and said: "Yeah, that is you!" When Earlene saw her, she wasn't surprised at all. She knew that Ernie had the hots for her ever since church last Sunday. And now, her history of knowing Peaches from church and seeing her Grandma's house spoke volumes. "Yeah, that's that two-dollar ho." And Angie said: "Yeah. That's the girl from church who's always trying to act all sanctified.

Peaches was offended by their snide comments, so she blasted back, saying, "I ain't no Ho, Bitch!" But before Angie and Earlene could tune her ass up, Ernie jumped in to defend her: "Leave her alone! You always trying to start some trouble, Earlene!" But it didn't end there.

"I know you didn't call me a Bitch—Bitch! You're out here running around with this Slut, Yolanda. The whole world knows, she's a community property ho. And you, you ain't nothing but a goodie-two-shoe acting ho." Then Earlene looked at Kim and Angie and said, "Lets kick their Asses yall!

But, regaining her consciousness just in time to stop another calamity, Grandma quickly came to her senses. She was tuned in to the last statement Earlene made, and she slowly pushed her 6- foot frame up and out of the chair and got to her feet. She said: "If anybody's going to do any Ass Kicking around here it's going to be Me."

That's when, everybody in the room tried to leave—they all headed for the door. But, Miss Ella caught them off guard when she whistled from her mouth a loud, crisp command for them to stop. She said: "Everybody Freeze! Freeze! get back in here! I ain't through with yall." Then she turned to look at Ernie and said: "What's going on here?" Ernie started babbling, "Ain't nothing going on, Grandma. We was just having some fun playing cards, that's all." She said, "Is that why I saw beer cans and wine bottles all over my living room, boy. Do you think I'm a fool? And you been smoking reefer in my house too!"

She pause in silence for a moment, and then she asked him: "Boy, don't you have one a baby already? And, I heard you got another girl pregnant!" "Naw, Grandma, that baby ain't mine." "Boy, shut up. It's the same story on a different day with you. You kids are just babies. Babies making Babies—that's what you are. You're too young to be fornicating, especially in my house!"

"You're seventeen years old, boy, and you're gonna have two babies to take care of before you're eighteen. You don't have a job, a pot to piss in, or a window to throw it out of. Boy, it's time to get something on your mind—and the same goes for you Monty."

Ernie was speechless, but he did manage to tell his Grandma that he was sorry, and there was no doubt that he was embarrassed. He just took what his Grandmother had to say and held his head down like he was ashamed.

Next, standing in front of her with scraggly hair and wrinkled blouses were the two girls. She looked them over and said: "Yolanda, what in the Hell are you two doing in my house. You're from the West End—down on 14th street. Don't think I don't know who you are—I know your mama, (but only the lord knows who your daddy is, she mumbled) And you! Ain't you Reverend Kimble's daughter?"

Peaches held her head up and spoke softly, "Yes Mam." Miss Ella shook her head and mumbled to herself, "well, lord have mercy, ain't this a blip. I know your mama would whoop your ass if she knew you were over here."

Then she laid down the law. "Now here this," she said, "These boys are here to learn how to live a Christian way of life and learn lessons from the Bible—not the kind of lessons you want to teach them. They're going to know who they are, and where they come from when they leave this house. "Now, if I catch nan one of you in my house again without my permission you're gonna be sucking your supper through a plastic straw for the rest of your natural life. Got it! Now go on, get out of here!"

Well, not long after the girls made their way out the front door, Lee and Leroy came stumbling through. They had been gone all day scouting the neighborhood, meeting new people, and getting their swerve on. Fortunately, Miss Ella wasn't around to smell their ninety-proof breath. And naturally, all of them had stories to tell each other.

Yet and still, at this time of the evening all of them were hungry, and bedtime was growing near. So, before they told their stories, they indulged on bologna and government cheese sandwiches and washed them down with a big glass of Kool-Aid. After they ate, they all had a chance to talk about their adventuresome day.

They matched stories about their encounter with the half-man/half-cow; Ernie and Monty boasted about the Freaky-Deaky time they had with Peaches and Yolanda, and Lee and Leroy talked about the girls they met, which included the girls they should-have, would-have, and could-have got it on with.

But, to put a cap on the night, AJ told them a joke about a, 'The girl in a wheelchair.' He said: "There was this quadriplegic girl, and she was sitting in a wheelchair next to a swimming pool. Well, a friend of hers heard her crying one day and walked up to her and asked her why she was crying. The girl told him "Because don't nobody love me" and the friend told her that he loved her, and she smiled and cheered up. And the next day, the friend saw her sitting by the pool crying again. So, he asked her what she was crying about now. And the girl said, "because don't nobody ever kiss me." So, the friend gives her a kiss, and she smiles and cheers up. So, the day after that, the friend sees her sitting by the pool crying again. So, he asked her what are you crying about today. And the girl says, "because don't nobody ever fuck me." So, the friend grabs hold of the girl's wheelchair and rolls her over to the deep end of the pool and dumps her ass in the water, and he says: "You're Fucked Now!"

CHAPTER TWELVE

THE STAR-SPANGLED EXPLOSION

They got a long, restful night of sleep last night, but the next morning they woke up to the sound of gunfire. It riddled through the neighborhood streets, and at the same time, it served as an alarm clock.

It was the 4th of July, and either that sudden burst of gunfire was an indication of the country's celebration of independence or a drive-by shooting. Either way, they knew they had to get up to get started with a day of festivities.

Miss Ella and Riley were up at 6 am as usual, and so was Samantha. She was in the habit of getting up early to eat breakfast and give her leftover food to Rah-Mel, but today was different, her duties today included helping out in the kitchen with the other girls.

Everyone in the house was needed to help get things ready for the backyard cookout. This was a big day for them. Aunt Ella had slabs of ribs and whole chickens cut up in the kitchen sink; Riley and Alvin were in the backyard filling up a barrel-grill with wood and charcoal.

Miss Ella was in the kitchen making decisions about who was going to help her prepare the food and clean the house—both inside and outside. In addition to those duties, there was an endless amount of things to do.

Anyway, Alvin got things started when he popped the trunk of his car open and pumped up the volume on his James Brown CD to get everyone in the groove.

And sure enough, the good spirits that the music put them in made it easier for them to clean, cook, sing and dance. But the super soul groove that James Brown put him in was eventually overturned, and the majority rule voted to change it to a Hip-Hop groove. So, Tu Pac, Biggie Smalls, and Snoop-Dog became the preferred artist of choice.

The music brought them closer together; they bonded like families should. And as one would presume, it made Aunt Ella very happy.

THE DRAMA BEGINS

A few hours later, all the hard work was done. Tables were set up, folding chairs were brought up from the basement, and oriental lanterns were strung up across the yard from one end to the other.

Food was cooking in the oven and on top of the stove, and Alvin and Riley took turns cooking meat on the grill while they quenched their thirst drinking ice-cold beer.

As soon as the girls did all their work inside, they went outside to chill with the boys. But, as they all gathered around the picnic tables waiting on a cool breeze to come their way—there was none, so they sat there suffering from the heat--hot, sweaty, and thirsty. But after several minutes of sitting in the same spot, without even the hint of a breeze coming, they moved the table under a tree to get some shade. And, to complement that idea was the idea to cool off by getting ice-balls from the basement freezer.

Well, that worked for a while, but it really wasn't enough to cool their hot body temperatures. So, a final option popped into the minds A.J. and Chunk. They quietly disappeared from the group, but they were later spotted peeping out the third-floor window.

A minute or two later, those two scoundrels 'set it off.' The first throw was a direct hit. A.J. busted his dad in the back of his head with a water balloon. Then Chunk raised up and threw the next one. It was a direct hit too—right in his Grandpa Riley's chest. After they hit them, they laid back down on the floor to get out of sight and laughed their devilish little asses off. The other kids were stunned when they saw what happened, but, at the same time, they were amused to the point of laughter.

Although, not so amused was Alvin and Riley. Alvin was pissed, and so was his dad. Alvin grabbed the back of his head and shouted, 'Son-of-a-bitch!' his first thought was that he had got shot in the head, but he soon realized that it was water on his head-- not blood. And, Uncle Riley thought it was all over for his ass too, but he saw the busted balloon laying on the ground in front of him and realized that somebody's up to some shit.

But it didn't stop there. It seems that those two little shits had been planning this all night long. They had a washtub filled with water balloons set aside for this moment. And, with all fun intended they continued their disruptive, distribution process by bombing whoever they could from the third-floor window.

Those two water-balloon assassins worked from that third-floor window with the skill, precision, and tenacity of two professional hit men. They would pop-up, throw their balloon, hit their target, and get back down and out of sight so that no-one could identify which one of them hit them.

Earlene was next to feel the sting of a balloon bursting on her back. She cringed from the cold water running down her back, and shouted: "Oh, Hell No!" Then Kim took two hits to the back of her head that knocked her into a state of double-vision. It had her staggering back and forth so much that she fell on Angie.

Right after that, they heard Leon laughing like a hyena--but not for long. The aerial precision displayed next had D.A. and Popsicle laughing at Leon, because at that moment he was double-attacked. Chunk threw a balloon that screw-balled Leon right between his teeth and AJ backed him up with a balloon that busted right upside his head.

Thus, as the terrorist balloon threats continued. The civilian population below scattered and scrambled around in a frenzy. They were helplessly at the mercy of the attackers and forced to use garbage-can tops to ward off the incoming barrage of balloons.

However, just like two commanders of a task force, Riley and Alvin came up with a plan to fight back. Alvin ran to his car and pulled out their secret weapon. Inside the large paper bag that he brought back with him were all kinds of fireworks—firecrackers, cherry-bombs, roman-candles, sparklers, and M-80's—the closest explosive to dynamite that can be legally sold as a commercial commodity.

Well, with no time wasted, and like two foot-soldiers on a combat mission, they quickly attacked the third-floor window. The first assault came from a round of firecrackers. Uncle Riley manned the fire from his lighter while Alvin lit a stringer of 50 of the volatile projectiles and skillfully tossed them through the third-floor window.

Immediately after landing on the floor between the two insurgents, the sound from that room resonated like machine-gun fire. Scared shit-less, A.J. and Chunk hit the floor and stayed there until it was over. Even Rah-Mel went berserk. He was climbing the walls of his cage when he heard the firecrackers exploding in rapid succession.

But that assault alone didn't get those two courageous soldiers to deviate from their established course of action one iota; it only intensified their savage instinct to vilify their subjects even more. So, with wild abandon, they pummeled one water-bomb after another directly beneath the window in a ceaseless effort to force the two hostiles (Uncle Riley and Alvin) into a new position.

Their counter-assault was devastating. It was a gloriously, magnificent defeat that could have been recorded in the log book of water-balloon history. There are no words that can describe the assault, other than to say that, no self-respecting duck would have been caught in a situation of this magnitude. Alvin and his dad were soaked from head to toe.

The others witnessed this brutal assault go on right in front of them, and from then on, a sense of retaliation overwhelmed all of them. Because now, it was an all-out war.

Ernie and Monty hooked up the garden hose laying at the bottom of the basement door and attached a spray nozzle to the other end of it; it was definitely going to be needed if this battle was going to continue on this level. D.A. Leon and Popsicle were grabbing any and everything that they could find on the battlefield ground to throw at them—sticks, bottles, and rocks.

Half of the girls went on a tactical mission up the stairs to the third floor to surprise attack and beat the hell out of them, and the other half stood on the ground selling wolf-tickets trying to draw their fire so Ernie and Monty could blast them with the hose.

Nonetheless, in between and in the meantime, Uncle Riley and Alvin had made it to a safe haven behind the huge Maple tree beside the grill. Mad as hell, sopping wet, and dripping with nullification from the mouth, Uncle Riley opened that bag of fireworks and looked inside for something that would blast their asses to the sky.

He said, "Give me those goddamn m-80's!" Alvin said, damn daddy! Your going to blow the whole damn house down!" Uncle Riley said, "I don't give a shit. Do you see what those little Mutha-fuckers did to me? I'll blow those little sum-bitches to kingdom come. Tell the lord to meet their souls in heaven; cause I'm gonna cover their asses with dirt when I'm through em".

A.J. and Chunk were totally unaware of their new strategy; nonetheless, Alvin and Uncle Riley moved into position to perpetuate their new assault. They cautiously approached the third- floor window to a point where they knew the projectiles would enter the window without obstruction and deliver the greatest impact. They made it to the house and positioned themselves; undetected by neither of the balloon-bombing bandits. Seconds later-- 5,4.3,2.1—pssssssst—pssssst--swish.... -ta—dump, ta—dump.

The miniature explosive packs landed in the middle of the floor hissing like two cobras. A.J. and Chunk saw both of the mini-charged explosives land on the floor and their eyes bulged with fright. Their first thought was to get the hell out the room. But, the sound of the banging and hollering on the other side of the door from the girls trying to get in let them know that they were in big trouble.

Besides that, the door was blocked by tables, chairs, a dresser, and an old trunk to keep the enemy out.

This was definitely a good time to panic, because after they looked at the door they looked at each other; then they looked at the open window. And, a split-second later they busted a move towards it.

It looked like a scene right out of an action Jackson movie after those two m-80's went "KA-Boom! KA-Bam" The momentum they had running toward the window was intensified by the thrust of the explosion. It sent them flying out of the third-floor window hollering through an unbelievable flight " Awe............. Shit..........!" They looked like two sky-divers with no parachutes.

Fortunately, they were lucky to have made it all the way to the maple tree in the middle of the yard, and even more fortunate to have landed on the picnic table that was underneath it.

Anyway, the ground troops were awestruck when they saw A.J. and Chunk fly through the air and topple down through those tree branches. When they saw the two wounded warrior's lifeless bodies laying there on the table they thought they were dead. And when Aunt Ella saw the little jackasses laying there in a state of catatonia she shouted "Oh, Lord Have Mercy!..." because she thought they were dead too. But her loud shouting must have jolted them back into consciousness because they slowly began moving around.

This was remarkable feat that everyone just witnessed was one in which a few of the head Bible-toting cousins thought was a miracle. Kim, Angie, and Tamara took the time to praise the Lord and applaud their survival. They were so exuberant and exalted by their survival that they decide to rejoice. They clapped their hands, stomped their feet, and started singing:

"We gonna jump down, turn around—pick-a-bail of cotton-- Jump up jump down—pick-a-bail of hay—Oh Lordy...., Pick-a-bail of cotton—Oh lordy......., pick-a-bail of hay..."

"Me and My Cousins gonna jump down, turn around—pick-a-bail of cotton-- Jump up jump down—pick-a-bail of hay—Oh Lordy......, Pick-a-bail of cotton—Oh lordy......., pick-a-bail of hay..."

"We gonna jump down, turn around—pick-a-bail of cotton-- Jump up jump down—pick-a-bail of hay—Oh Lordy...., Pick-a-bail of cotton—Oh lordy......., pick-a-bail of hay..."

"Me and My Cousins gonna jump down, turn around—pick-a-bail of cotton-- Jump up jump down—pick-a-bail of hay—Oh Lordy...., Pick-a-bail of cotton—Oh lordy......., pick-a-bail of hay..."

They sang, clapped their hand, stomped their feet, and strutted around the backyard like they were on an Alabama plantation, right up until the time that Miss Ella said: let's eat.

CHAPTER THIRTEEN

THE DRIVE-BY DROP-OFF

Uncle Hump had a raw and sometimes brutal demeanor about him; he spoke his mind. He said what was natural for him to say, and he was shameless after he said it. But, most of the time he was a fun-loving, easy-going guy.

It completely surprised Miss Ella when her younger 'menace-to-society' brother showed up at the cookout. And although it wasn't his intended destination; he wound up there as the result of a 'drive-by-drop off.'

Uncle Hump was a passenger in his x-wife's car until he pissed her off. And, while in the vicinity of his sister's house, she barreled down the back alley to where she lived and told him to get the fuck out. After that, she pulled off kicking back dirt and gravel from beneath her tires. She created a cloud of dust after she dropped him off, and at the same time, she shouted every obscenity in a Black woman's vocabulary at him. But, Uncle Hump was cool about it. He just stood there in the dust, shrugged his shoulders, and said: "I can't stand your black ass either, 'You Bitch!'

He got the nickname 'Hump' because of his reputation being in brawls in back-alley's, pool halls, and bars around town. And, more or less, because of the king size knot on his forehead.

Well, soon after he was abandoned, he shook the dust off his clothes and straightened the feather in the brim of his hustler's hat. Then he opened the gate to the backyard and walked inside.

Then he followed the cloud of smoke next to the grill and waited for it to clear. Alvin and Uncle Riley were burning the last pieces of meat they were cooking. But, before he approached them, as usual, he checked his package with one hand and swung his arm synchronously to his hustler's 'Kimble' to show them that he was still a 'Mack.'

"Hey, what's up, brother-in law, how you doing nephew?" "Hey, what's going on Unc, how've you been? He said: "nephew I've been dong fine. You know how I do it. I keep my powder dry, I keep my dick hard, and watch the World Turn,' baby; how about you?"

Uncle Riley turned to look at him and was quick to ask him: "Nigga, when did they let you out of jail?" Hump said, "Don't you worry about that, nigga, I'm here right now ain't I-- Signed, sealed, and delivered, Baby! If you 'free your mind, your ass will follow.' That's something that a old country ass nigga like you don't know nothing about." And in the same breath he held out his hand and said, "let me hold something?" But Riley was even quicker when he said "Fuck You Nigga!" and turned his back on him.

All of a sudden, Hump's grand-daughter, Sparkle jumped on his back and wrapped her arms around his neck. But, Leon wasn't so charmed when he saw his legendary Grandfather. It was an awkward moment for him, and one in which his distinctive laughter wouldn't be heard. From past experiences, he knew that as soon as he showed up, he'd make him a promise, tell him a lie and be gone again. So, he didn't even take the time to be bothered with him.

Aunt Ella was of a similar opinion about her brother. He had been a disappointment to her and the family many times before. She was standing on the porch with an apathetic look on her face when she saw him. But he still looked her up and down while she was sweeping off the porch. So as he walked towards her he immediately heard the sarcasm in her voice: "Well, well, well, the fugitive has returned." But, being the silky-smooth kind of player he was, his special brand of charm was accompanied with a calm response: "Now is that any way to talk to your favorite baby brother, Sis? Come on now, wobble your big ass down those steps and show me some love."

Well, as much as she wanted him to feel the disgust she had for him, she laughed and gave in to his undignified brand of charm--she made her way down the steps and gave him a hug. After that, Uncle Hump turned into his wild, fun-loving, playful self. He grabbed each one of his great-nieces by their hands and swung them around and around until they couldn't walk straight when he let go of them.

After that he showed his great nephews his boxing style--he playfully sparred with all of them. He threw light punches at them; however, he intentionally landed one or two hard punches every now and then to show them that he still had some sting in his punches. But when it came to Popsicle, he landed a stiff blow to his chest, but Popsicle got so mad that he countered with a hard right hook to Hump's jaw and drew blood from the corner of his mouth. Hump stood there silence for a second or two and wiped the blood from his mouth Then stuck his other hand in his back pocket feeling for his razor and said, "Awe Shit! Now I got ta cut ya."

But, as quick as a flash, Popsicle pulled his knife from back of his shoe and flicked open and squared of with him. He said, "Come on, Bust a move, you old Mutha-Fucka!" But, during that brief moment, Uncle Hump had a flashback; he saw himself standing there doing the exact same thing forty years ago—brave, arrogant, and foolish. So, he just shook his head, laughed and said, "somebody put on some music."

After the music started, the soul-train showdown began. Uncle Hump brought the funk back to town. He showed them how to do the 'dog, and the cosmic slop, and the bump'. Then they showed him how to do the running man, the wobble, the butterfly, and the cabbage-patch.

Finally, they voted on the 1st, 2nd, and 3rd place winners of the Soul-train dance line and argued over who did what dance the best. And as such, the fun lasted until sundown--up until the time that they set off fireworks...

THE GREAT ESCAPE

As darkness fell, Uncle Riley set off his fireworks, and all of a sudden, the sound of fireworks and firecrackers exploding could be heard everywhere. The night sky was filled with a colorful rainbow of lights bursting throughout the neighborhood.

However, barely noticeable, sitting across the ally in a big, black Cadillac were two men with the driver-side window pulled halfway down. As soon as Uncle Hump saw the car sitting there, he ducked down as low as he could get to get out of sight. And right after the bright sky returned to darkness, he made a B-line for the back door and went inside the house. And, as soon as the night sky lit up again, the men in the car noticed that Hump was nowhere in sight.

It soon came to pass that these two men were gangsters from Detroit; they had been watching the house for a long time now. Needless to say, they were after Hump, for who knows what. Furthermore, immediately following Uncle Hump's sudden disappearance, A.J. was so curious that he followed him in the house to find out what was going on. But when he got inside the house, Hump came out of the dark hallway and muffled A. J.'s mouth; he pulled him in the hallway with him and in a low, desperate whisper, he asked A.J. if he knew anybody with a car.

Meanwhile, the men got out the car and walked up to the fence in the backyard. They had on black three-piece suits and they were wearing Gangster style fedoras. When they reached the gate, one of the men asked: "Does anybody here know Hump Wilson?" But there was a dead silence for several seconds. And with no answer to his question, he asked again. Speaking louder this time, he asked: "Does anybody here know Hump Wilson?" Then Uncle Riley walked toward Rah-Mel's cage in plain view of the men and answered their question with the question: "Who wants to know?"

During that same moment, Alvin took it as a queue to get everybody inside the house. He got up and walked toward the house while telling everyone to go inside. And, with little resistance, they felt the stern sense of seriousness in his voice; they all went inside without questions. After everyone was through the door, he walked to the back of his car and unlocked the trunk and stood next to it.

The two men were still standing at the fence at a loss for words to answer the question Uncle Riley asked them. But eventually, both of them spoke at the same time—each with a different answer; stumbling over the right words to say. And with that being the case, the only reasonable answer they could respond with was that, "We're just some old friends of his from out of town, and we wanted to stop by to see how he was doing—that's all."

Uncle Riley and Alvin had already surmised that these two men weren't cops, and they sure as hell weren't his friends. From the way they were dressed, they were either businessmen, or a couple of hit-men after Hump for something; it was obvious to them that their latter thought was the correct one.

And as such, assuming their latter thought was the correct one, Uncle Riley cited them some profound words of wisdom. He told them: "Look here, the only thing I'd like to see more than fireworks lighting up in the sky tonight, is the fire I'm gonna light up under your asses if you don't get off my Goddamn property, right fucking Now!"

Then he opened the gate to Rah-Mel's cage and shouted: "Kill Rah-Mel!" And Rah-Mel he took off running towards the fence barking ferociously. When Alvin heard Rah-Mel's barking he opened the trunk of his car and grabbed his gun and waited for his daddy to make the next move.

Startled by the sudden surprise, both men reached inside their suit coats and pulled revolvers from their shoulder holsters and pointed them at Rah-Mel. But in the midst of the distraction, Uncle Riley had quickly reached inside a compartment on top of Rah-Mel's doghouse and pulled out a 12-gauge shot-gun.

He had it aimed at the men, and he angrily shouted, "If you shoot my dog, you'll be some dead Mutha-fuckers right where you stand!" This time, Alvin was standing right alongside his daddy with his nine, cocked, loaded, and pointed at both men.

And just like that, the gangsters attitudes changed when they saw the odds stacked against them. They nervously muttered, "O k. O k, O k old man—don't shoot—do you hear me, don't shoot, we're leaving-- we're leaving right now! Alright!" And they hurried back across the alley and got in their car and drove off.

Immediately following their hasty departure, AJ was heard coming through the front door. He had taken Uncle Hump out the front door and across the street to a neighbor's house, and accordingly, Uncle Hump promptly finagled the neighbor into driving him across the river into Kentucky. Anyway, after everybody went through that stressful situation, there was a sigh of relief.

But the worst part of the night was seeing the long, sad look of disappointment on Sparkle's face knowing that her Grandfather had left without even saying good-by. However, Leon was used to this sort of thing happening. He knew for certain that his Grandfather was going to be on the run again, and frankly, he didn't give a shit.

CHAPTER FOURTEEN

HOT CONFLICTS

Uncle Hump wasn't seen or heard from for the remainder of the summer, and despite them knowing about the ordeals and controversy that were part of his life, he would always be remembered for bringing them a certain amount of joy at a special time in their lives.

Anyway, as their summertime experience continued, one hot conflict after another continued to occur. Furthermore, the pattern of mischief and mayhem that prevailed was supplemented by the blazing hot temperature during the month of July. However, the hot temperature can't diminish the fact that a lot of these conflicts were the direct result of the vengeful thoughts that a select few family members were harboring against each other.

Miss Ella wanted these children to be knowledgeable of who their cousins and the immediate family members were. Bringing cousins together for the summer had been had become a matter of tradition in this family, along with the process of getting kids accustomed to going to church.

Therefore, during the next four weeks, these kids attended several denominations of churches: Baptist, Methodist, Lutheran, and Holiness. Some of them were so tired of going to church that every time they got on that bus, they felt like a group of traveling Jesuits.

At times they were bored out of their minds sitting in church all day long. And at times, it seemed like some of the people in church gave unbelievable testimonials. Certain members would give the same testimonial about how God intervened in the lives of their sons or daughters and made them miss a plane or a train ride that later on crashed with no survivors.

And sometimes the services were so comical that some of them couldn't stop laughing. Especially when the preacher used street slang to get his message across to the younger members in church. At times they'd laugh until tears rolled from their eyes.

Furthermore, at this point in time in their lives, the most profound lessons they learned from going to church every week were that: the Methodist preacher were liquor drinking alcoholic; the Holiness preacher was fried chicken-biscuit and gravy sopping glutton; the Baptist preacher was a, two faced, womanizing adulterer, and that the Lutheran church was spooky as hell!

Anyway, when they got back home, it was plain to see that these kids weren't angles. Aunt Ella's big, spacious home had become a place where they could be free and run wild. Thus, their usual mode of behavior resumed its course. Therefore, incident after incident of mischief and unbelievable pranks and were carried on behind Miss. Ella's back--around the clock.

The first incident reached a 99.9 on the 'mischief meter.' It happened on a sweltering, hot afternoon. Popsicle was craving one of those sweet cherry ice-balls in the basement deep-freezer, and as such, he took off on his own walking through the back hallway toward the basement. Well, his timing couldn't have been better. His archenemy, Kim, the queen of the oatmeal fight, just happened to be in the kitchen--filling up Dixie Cups with Kool-Aid. She was placing them on a flat metal pan and was just about ready to take them to the basement deep freezer.

Popsicle was standing behind the half-opened door watching her through the crack of the door, and naturally, a rotten thought crossed his mind. So, he stood there patiently and watched and waited for her to finish. And when she finished, she picked up the pan and slowly walked towards the door without spilling a drop of Kool-Aid: so far so good. Then, she went through the door and got one foot firmly planted on the first step. But, as soon as she put her other foot on the step "Wham" Popsicle pushed the door and slammed it against her hefty behind and it knocked her off balance and sent her tumbling down a flight of twenty steps-- screaming at the top of her lungs.

Unfortunately, no-one could her screams but Popsicle, and when he did, the rotten creep felt a sense of pleasure and satisfaction. And as far as he was concerned, hearing her yell like that was sweeter than any cherry-ice-ball could have ever been.

The cups of Kool-Aid went flying in the air when she tumbled down that long flight of steps to the cement floor. The only sounds that could be heard in that basement were the sounds of the wooden steps cracking, and her yelling: "Awe............................Shit!" All the way down to the bottom.

Amazingly, the booms and bangs and terror-filled screams didn't escape Samantha's hearing. She was in the backyard with Rah-Mel when she heard the tragic moment transpire. So, she immediately went to the basement window to see what had happened.

She was surprised to see Kim sitting at the bottom step, slumped over in a daze; covered from head to toe with cherry Kool-Aid. And she could tell by her slow movement that she was hurt, and fortunately she was still alive, so with no-time wasted, she ran to her rescue.

Meanwhile, that black Hearted buzzard inconspicuously fled from the crime scene and ran into D.A. in the next room. So giggling like a rat, he and stopped to tell him about his dastardly deed; then they both enjoyed a fiendish laugh about his appalling act of terrorism.

Kim nor Sam knew who was responsible, but they had a strong suspicion, and they knew that it wasn't an accident. Therefore, after clearing her head, and the crime scene, they brainstormed and formulated a plan to find out who was responsible and how to get even.

Meanwhile, the third floor of the house was rocking with the sound of hip-hop music. It was so loud that it blasted through the floor and down the steps to where the two co-conspirators were collaborating. When they heard the music, they were ensued by a spirit of exploration, and naturally, feeling embolden with confidence, they went upstairs to satisfy their curiosity.

When they got there, they walked in to see Danielle and Sparkle smoking Cigarettes and sipping on a fifth of Long Island Iced Tea. Deeper still, they were dressed up like "Salt n Pepper' and singing: "What a man, what a man, what a man, what a mighty good man." And from the sound of their slurred singing, you could tell they were drunk. Sparkle was standing in front of a long, stand-up mirror putting on makeup and jewelry and brushing her hair to match Salt-n-Pepper's style.

And, as soon as Danielle saw them, she invited them in. She was lounged in a reclining chair with the bottle of iced tea in her hand. Furthermore, she was wearing a short skirt and she had one of her legs cocked up over the arm of the chair with her panties showing.

She said, "Hey Popsicle, do you want-a Pop this Thang? I got some chocolate puddin for you, baby. Umm, its and it's sweet too." Then Sparkle flirted with D.A. She bent over in front of the mirror-- wearing tight booty shorts, Then she started twerking and jiggling her behind like a bowl of Jello. She said: "Hey D.A., you wanna ride my pony. All you got to do is hop on and smack that ass."

The only thing that kept their jaw's from dropping to the floor, and their faces from turning red, black and bluer than they were, was when Tamara overheard them from the next room. She busted in and said, "You Fools! Those are your cousins!" Then, she commenced scolding them about their shameful behavior. But due to their inebriated condition, they felt no shame-- they just giggled and laughed at her to the point of pissing her off. And as such, her lecture fell on deaf ears; she bored them into sleeping off their state of intoxicated foolishness. Then she made D.A. and Pop promise to say nothing about the incident to anyone.

SAMANTHA'S SURPRISE

Anyway, the following morning marked a turning point for, Samantha because she finally got her long-awaited phone call from her Grandmother. The call put her in good spirits and back on track, because after she heard her Grandma's voice over the phone, she turned into the sweet, loving, temperamental, spoiled brat that had been waiting to come out.

She was the youngest of all the cousins in the family, and for a long time she had felt awkward being around them; however, now it was easier for her to adapt to her situation. Furthermore, she stuck to Miss Ella like glue, and she didn't hesitate to tell any of the boys just what she thought of them. As a matter of fact, she gained a sense of power that was indirectly backed Miss Ella, Uncle Riley, and Rah-Mel.

On the flip side, D.A. was having a fantastic time adapting to this new environment. He took to it like a fish takes to water. His personality blended in with all the other boys in the house. However, the other boy's subtle pranks, horse play, and ridiculous antics were emerging to the point of pissing their female cousins off. However, it didn't take long time for all of them to figure out that all of their female cousins had PHD's in Bullshit management.

On another note, several weeks had passed since Earlene's bicycle was totally destroyed by the house nemesis, A.J. But, her Uncle Alvin was true to his word; he kept his promise by buying her a bran-new ten-speed that afternoon. When he called her to come out back to see it, her face lit up. She ran up to him, stopped, looked at the bike and asked him if it was for her. Without saying a word, he handed her a key-chain lock and said, only if you promise to keep it locked up when you're not using it. She said I promise, I promise, Uncle Alvin and thank you so much. She wrapped her arms around him and gave him a big hug. Then she jumped on the bike and took it for a spin around the block.

While she was riding, she was as happy as she could be. Her Uncle Alvin had kept his word, and she was ever so grateful. However, she was also mindful about what had happened to her other bicycle, and she thought to herself that there was no way in hell that, that (rat-ass A.J. was going to steal this bike).

In the meantime, from the kitchen window, A.J. witnessed his dad giving Earlene that new bicycle, and it filled him with envy and contempt. He turned to Chunk, who was watching too and said, "Ain't this about a bitch! That nappy head heifer got a new bike from my dad, and all I got to ride is that raggedy-ass piece of shit that I've had for the last five years." A.J. was pissed, and Chunk knew the flavor of the Kool-Aid in the back of his mind-- he also knew that A.J. was going to get him caught up in some shit with that girl.

    Well anyway, the only one Earlene would trust with her bike was Angie. They took turns riding here and there throughout the day. To the store, to the hair salon, to the playground, and through the park; that was the basic limit of their destinations. And at every turn, A.J. was there to beg them to let him ride it —just around the corner, or to the store and right back, so he'd say. And every time he asked, their flat-out answer was "Hell to the Goddamn No!

CHAPTER FIFTEEN

The last week being at Miss Ella's house was nearly here. To most of them the time flew by overnight. However, their random acts rambunctious behavior hadn't changed at all.

Furthermore, Miss Ella's health wasn't in the best of all conditions. She had been falling into bad health for some time now, yet and still, regardless of her health, she held on to what she felt obligated to do. Her spirit was still on course, and in her mind, she was determined to play an integral part in the reassessment of these kids lives. But, until that time arrived, the gravity of the situation that had been underway remained the same.

THE AVENGERS

August 8th, Monday morning. Kim and Samantha had finally came up with a plan to execute their revenge. Nearly a week had passed since Kim's tumble down the basement steps. However, it naturally came to pass that Kim's suspicion about Popsicle being the one responsible for her copious venture down the basement steps was worth following through with Therefore, she and Samantha kept their ears open and their mouths shut about the incident, and by doing that, they overheard conversations of Popsicle and D.A. talking about what he did--and thus, the truth came out; what she heard pissed her off. Every time she saw the shit-eating grins and smirks on Popsicle and D.A.' faces when they talked about it made her boiling mad.

Well, anyway, today was payback day; Kim and Samantha set out to do what they needed to do. They knew their upcoming offensive right down to the right timing and whatever else they needed to do to execute their plan one. Their plan basically involved luring Popsicle to the basement door and the simple element of surprise. The knowledge of what could be expected from that rotten rat after the plan was in action was inevitable.

Anyway, later that afternoon, she and Samantha set their trap with a game of 'follow the dollar.' They knew that that money snatching, ice-ball loving, Popsicle would be going through the back hallway past the basement pretty soon; he always went that way to stay out of Aunt Ella's sight to avoid a confrontation with her.

And with that being the case, they set out to see if the ten-fresh one-dollar bills they had saved for bait; a bottle of dish washing liquid, a stiff frying pan, and one of the most gruesome, grotesque zombie mask they could find would do the job they planned to do.

Well, the plan started from the bottom to the top with Samantha in the process of laying dollar bills on every other basement step all the way to the top. Kim stayed in the basement with the zombie mask waiting for just the right time to put it on and lay down inside Grandma's double-wide deep freezer.

So, when Sam reached the top step of the stairs, she stuck a bill halfway underneath the partially opened basement door. Thus, the trap was set.

From past experience, they knew that it would be a cold day in hell before that money snatching runt could resist this temptation, and as such, he fell right into their trap like a piece in a jigsaw puzzle. Samantha sat at the kitchen table, armed with a bottle of liquid dish soap when she heard the basement door creep open, and so far everything was going just like they predicted.

When Popsicle saw the dollar bill sticking from underneath the basement door, his eyes lit up. And when he opened the basement door and saw the other dollar bills on the steps; his eyes sparkled like diamonds, so he went all the way down the steps and picked up each and every one of them.

So, as he reached the bottom step, he picked up the last dollar and stuck it in his pocket, and, from that point on Popsicle felt pretty good-- he just made ten dollars and didn't have to run away from anybody to keep it. So, as good as he felt, he looked over at the deep freezer and said to himself 'why not,' a cherry ice-ball would taste good with this free money. So, he walked over to the deep freezer and opened it up.

And right after he did, he screamed like a sissy and pissed in his pants because Kim sat up inside that deep freezer with that zombie mask on and spoke to him like she was the living dead. She said: "Do You Feel Lucky Punk! Huh? Do You?"

Well, as soon as Samantha heard the scream, her job was to open the basement door and squirt the dish soap on all the steps. Well, she managed to get the top half of the steps squirted down, but, as fast as Popsicle was running, half of the steps was all she could manage to do. But, as soon as he reached the top half of the steps Popsicle lost his footing and slipped on that liquid soap and slid all the way down to the bottom.

Likewise, following his backslide, Popsicle got the ass-whooping of a lifetime. Kim was waiting there with that frying pan and she beat the living shit out of him with it. Every time he broke loose and ran up the steps to get away, he'd slide back down to the bottom and she'd beat him with wild, whirlwind swings with that frying pan.

Well, soon afterwards, D.A. showed up. He was looking for Popsicle, and as he came closer to the basement door he heard his merciless screams. Then he saw Samantha standing by the half-opened door giggling and smiling with glee. She was shouting instructions down the steps to Kim: "That's right, Kim. Beat the meat off that Rat! I bet he won't mess with you again."

By this time, Kim had taken off the mask so he could see who was going upside his head with that frying pan, and at the same time she told him: "I know it was you who pushed me down these steps last week, you little Fuckhead! And give me back my money!"

Nevertheless, after a few seconds of seeing his partner being beat into submission, D.A. mustered up enough nerve to enter that chamber of horror. Samantha tried her best to keep him out, but he struggled with her over the rights to the door and won. He immediately rushed to get down the steps to rescue him, but he had no way of knowing that the top half was covered with dish soap. And as such, when he reached the third step, he lost his footing and went on a bumpy roller coaster ride—he bounced down to the bottom of those steps right beside Popsicle.

Well, he was definitely feeling helpless and terrified when he reached the bottom, and he soon realized that he was about to receive an ass whooping right alongside Popsicle. But he managed to get to his feet and run back up the steps to the door. However, when he tried to open the door to get out, Samantha banged him in the head with the door the at the same time he was trying to open it. It caused him to slip and slide right back down to the bottom. She was having the time of her life, because every time she heard him make it to the top step, she banged him in the head with that door and made him slide back down to the bottom, and every time she did it, she screamed and hollered laughing.

But, after what seemed like hours of insurmountable pleasure for Samantha, D.A. finally broke through her defense. He managed to get a hand and an arm through the door to open it up and pull himself through. But, by the time he had gotten to his feet, Samantha had scrambled. She took off like a rocket-ship headed for the moon. By the time D.A. saw the tail end of that rocket-ship, it was flying through the kitchen and out the backdoor. So, with fury in his heart, he ran through the kitchen and out the backdoor only to see Samantha standing in the middle of the backyard next to Rah-Mel's cage.

Well, by this time, D.A. thought his chase was over. And although he was about ten yards away from grabbing her by the throat and shaking the shit out of her. But as he ran toward her, she casually opened the gate to Rah-Mel's cage and stood behind it.

And naturally, Rah-Mel sprang out of and growled at D.A.; showing him his long, pretty white teeth. And as such, D.A. immediately put on his breaks, and came to a Flintstone stop, but he still slid about three feet in front of the ravenous K-9. And, when he came to a complete stop, he immediately reversed his charge and started running in the opposite direction--that's when Samantha shouted: "Get him Rah-Mel!"

Rah-Mel got a hold of one of D. A's raggedy gym shoes and stripped it off his foot. Then, half-way up the back-porch steps he got hold of a pant leg and ripped it to pieces. Then, with his draws showing, Rah-Mel had his mouth wide open and was about to take a bite out of his ass when Tamara rushed out the back door and stuck the wood-handle of a mop in Rah-Mel's mouth. But Rah-Mel bit through it like it was a tooth-pick, so she turned it around and beat him off with the mop end, and that gave D.A. just enough time to crawl to the door and get inside the house.

Anyway, by the time these two fallen soldiers saw each other again, D.A. was stretched out on the kitchen floor next to the back door, and Popsicle had finally crawled up the basement steps and made his way into the hallway next to the kitchen floor. But, all they had the strength to do was look at each other with the agony of defeat written all over their faces.

CHAPTER SIXTEEN

OPERATION DOOR JAM

After Kim and Samantha served Popsicle and D.A. their sweet piece of justice that morning, later that afternoon, the mischief at the Walker house was on the rise again. The joke that A.J. planned to play on his father was in its developmental stage, but it was definitely coming into focus.

Alvin was waiting for a special part to be shipped to the auto store. His Cadillac had been down for a week and he was anxious to get it running again. That being the case, he was waiting on a phone call from the parts store to let him know that his part had came in.

Well, A.J. overheard the gist of this information and his mind was in the process of plotting a plan to perpetrate his mischief. Still being spiteful about his dad giving Earlene a new bicycle, he and Chunk paired up in a quest that would without a doubt piss him off. However, neither one of them counted on the fact that Grandpa Riley would be subjected to the silly, yet classic prank they had in store for him.

Rah-Mel's taste of freedom earlier that day must have filled him with the desire to be free from his cage again, because somehow he got loose. Evidently, Samantha didn't secure the lock on his cage properly when she put him back inside. But, he still must have climbed over or found an opening in the fence around the backyard.

Anyway, Rah-Mel was spotted running down the alley and through the neighborhood, and that meant that Riley and Alvin had a time-consuming task ahead of them. They had to hunt him down and bring him back home.

During this time span, A.J. and Chunk conspired to implement "Operation Door Jam." And as such, the first thing they set out to do was find two long pieces of rope. After they found them, they went to Grandpa Riley's car and opened the doors to his station wagon and ran the long pieces of rope underneath the seats-- from the passenger side to the driver's side, and they tied them to the front door handles. After that, they did the same thing to the back door handles. Then they rolled up all the windows and crawled out the back gate.

Well, soon after that, Alvin and Riley caught Rah-Mel and put him back in his cage, and that's when A.J. and Chunk went through with phase two of their plan. From across the alley to the backyard, A.J. used a neighbor's mobile phone to call the house. When Alvin heard the phone ringing and ran in the house to answer it. Then Chunk got on the phone and disguised his voice to make him think he was a salesman making an official call; he told him that he could come and pick up his part at the store.

And from across the alley, they watched Alvin rush out the back door and say, "Come on daddy my part just came in, let's go pick it up at the auto store." Well, from that point on, it looked like a scene from the Three Stooges. And the audience watching them was those two scamps across the alley--and they laughed their rotten asses off.

Uncle Riley was the first to open his door, and when he did, it opened up about six inches and slammed shut. Likewise, Alvin was doing the same thing at the same time, opening his door and having it pulled shut. At that moment, both of them were confused as hell. They didn't know what was happening, so they tried it again, and again and every time they tried to open their door, the other's door slammed shut. Then they tried the back doors, and again, the same thing happened.

It took a while, but after a few minutes of them looking like two dumb asses, Uncle Riley smelled some foul shit going on.

When they finally figured out what was happening, they heard laughing coming from behind the bushes across the alley. And then they knew that this kind of shit had A.J. and Chunk's name written all over it. When they took a closer look at the car, they saw the ropes attached to the door handles coming from underneath the seat. Uncle Riley looked at Alvin and said: "Well I Will Be Goddamn! Those rotten Mutha-fuckas."

Anyway, to make a long story short, Uncle Riley was so pissed off that he let Rah-Mel back out of his cage. He took him to the back gate and let him run free, all-the-while hoping that Rah-Mel would hunt them down and tare a new asses.

Well, after a few minutes, Rah-Mel spotted them, and they spotted Rah-Mel running towards them, so they took off like two runaway slaves. And, after a short chase down the alley and across the railroad tracks he caught up with them; they had climbed halfway up a tree, and they were holding on to the branches for dear life; Rah-Mel was at the bottom barking-- ready to rip them from limb to limb.

So, to teach them a lesson about fucking with him, Grandpa Riley let Rah-Mel babysit them for a while; which turned out to be half the night. But, when Miss Ella found out what had happened, and where they were, she as furious with Riley. She nearly had to beg him to go get Rah-Mel so the boys could come home.

Well, it took a while for her to break through Riley's stubbornness, but he eventually gave in. But, before he left the house, he stopped by the ice box to get Rah-Mel a treat to reward him for his obedience. Then walked on out the door. When he got to the tree, he patted Rah-Mel on his head and told him "Good Boy." Then he looked up and saw A.J. and Chunk still holding on to the branches in the tree. After that, he pulled a long strip of raw steak out of his overall's pocket; held it up in the air and said: "Do you boys see this. This is your ass." Then he tossed the steak to Rah-Mel and Rah-Mel devoured it in a few seconds. Then Riley looked up at the boys and said: "Did you see that. That's your ass if you ever fuck with me or my car again. Now, get out of that Goddamn tree and come on home!"

CHAPTER SEVENTEEN

HIP-HOP FEVER

Danielle and Sparkle went on a cross-town adventure later that night. Tamara noticed them missing at about 11:30. She didn't hear the usual snoring coming from their bedroom and she had a suspicion that something was wrong. So, she went to their room and pulled back the covers; there were piles of clothes shaped like two bodies in their beds. Therefore, it was obvious that those two girls had flew the coop.

Furthermore, Tamara found a flyer on the floor next to their beds. It was a much-needed clue to solve the mystery of their disappearance. It read: "All Night Skate Party 12:00—6:00 A.M. Golden Skates 1209 E. Kemper Rd Ages allowed--18-25—admission $2.00 at door. Contest prizes for best single, couple, and group skating competition. $300.00 for first prize winners, $200.00 for 2nd place, and $100.00 for 3rd"

Now, Tamara knew it all. The two hip-hop entertainers were on the other side of town at the skating rink showing off their skating talent. However, it didn't change the fact that neither one of those girls were 18. So as reluctant as she was to tell someone about it, she knew she had to. And that someone was Alvin.

When Tamara told him what was going on it was 12:30. And the only people rolling around at that time, other than Daniel and Sparkle was Alvin when he rolled over in his bed and told Tamara "Fuck Em!" But Tamara persisted in the matter. She screamed, yelled, and ridiculed him with the biggest guilt complex she could muster to get him out of that bed.

Anyway, during their ride to the rink, they both wondered how they could let two under-aged girls in without proper identification; however, when they got inside the rink and saw hey were dressed they understood why. They were dressed like two Hollywood moguls. They had on blonde wigs with a streak of purple dye in them; they had on designer sunglasses; black spandex leotards and to top it off, they rented red, high-top roller skates.

Well, Tamara spotted the bright red freckles on Danielle's face, and Sparkle's big, corn cob calves, and she was able to identify them. They were out on the floor shaking their groove-thang—swirling and twirling around in their roller skates.

So, they stood there and watch the show. All of them were good, and, with 10 other skating couples on the floor, the judges had a hard time declaring a first-place winner. These skaters were zig-zagging around that rink like professionals; doing all sorts of stunts—back-flips, cartwheels, splits, and 360-degree spins. They were skating forward, backwards, sideways--sliding through the legs and riding on the backs and shoulders of their partner's.

But, those two sixteen-year-old girls held their own. They did everything and anything the other skaters could do. Therefore, as it turned out, they didn't win the $300 first place prize, but they did win the $200 second place prize and a trophy. But, the contempt that came from some of the other couples was disheartening.

A couple of girls that knew Danielle and Sparkle knew that neither one of them was 18. Therefore, they contested their win on the grounds of being under age. When that news got out, there was slight uproar among some of the sour-grape losers, but it quickly simmered down. Because, despite the judges being notified of their ages, there were no other candidates in the competition that even came close to matching the points that Danielle and Sparkle had, so, the judges sustained their decision for the 2nd place prize regardless of their ages.

There was no doubt that the judges would have felt like hypocrites if they took back a second-place prize from the girls after their fair and square performance. They had obviously showed more talent than some of the older girls. But, there was still a group of girls who just wouldn't let it go. Thus, a can of worms was opened that turned into a real live smack down fight.

On the flipside, the girls may have won two hundred dollars and a trophy for second place, but it didn't elude from the fact that what they did was totally irresponsible; they left the house without letting anybody know their whereabouts. Alvin was upset with her because of what she and Sparkle had done. When the girls approached them, the fleeting look on his face let her know that she was going to face some sort of punishment.

Nevertheless, Alvin and Tamara had a seat while the girls returned their skates to the check-out counter. There was a long line when they got there, and there were three Amazon warriors standing there waiting-- the 'Arnold Sisters,' all of them were at least six feet tall and weighed over two hundred pounds. One of them approached Sparkle and said: "I know you. You're from Lincoln Heights." Sparkle said: "Yeah, so what." "Girl, you know you ain't hardly no eighteen." Sparkle said: "don't worry about it, we still won second place." After that, Danielle started to mouth off. "Yeah, at least we won second place. What place did you Ho's come in tonight?"

And that was just the right thing to say to piss those big heifers off because Danielle got hit in the mouth so hard that she back peddled halfway through a crowd of people--right back to where her daddy and Tamara were sitting. When Sparkle saw that Danielle was out of commission, she got scared and went wild swinging her skates back and forth at anyone she could hit. And to her surprise, she hit the oldest sister upside her head with one of her skates. Then the youngest and meanest sister of the bunch grabbed Sparkle from behind and held her while her older sister beat on her like she was a punching bag.

Well, Alvin was enraged when he saw Danielle's face. Blood was running out the side of her mouth, and she had a glassy look in her eyes. Furthermore, the girl that hit her was still on the warpath and headed straight towards her. But, Alvin suddenly jumped to his feet when he saw her coming. She was wolfing. She said: "I ain't no Ho little girl, and you better watch your mouth before I..." Bam! Before she could finish what she was saying, Alvin fired out and surprise attacked her. He took off full speed and close-lined her across the neck--she fell flat on her back. All she could do was look and wonder how in the hell she wound up on the floor.

After that windfall, they grabbed hold of Danielle and took her to the car. But, on the way out the door, they saw Sparkle being double-teamed by the other two sisters. But, Tamara told Alvin to go on-- take Danielle to the car; she was going to handle this. But, first things first, she said a short prayer. She said: "Lord, forgive my trespasses as I forgive those who trespass against me. And please, don't let me kill these two bitches."

Tamara walked up behind the oldest sister and tapped her on the shoulder. She said: "Stop beating on my cousin." But the girl just turned and looked down her nose at Tamara and ignored her. Then she turned around and wound up to give Sparkle another gut punch. However, in the midst of her doing so, Tamara tapped her on the shoulder again, but this time the girl made a sudden mojo move; she turned and swung on Tamara and missed, Tamara ducked the punch, and hit that girl in the face with a left-right combination so fast that it stunned her.

But, when the girl recovered, she got her bearings together and charged at Tamara like an out-of-control maniac. But, Tamara quickly side-stepped her and hit her upside her head with a hard right hook that made her lose her balance. The girl hit her head against a marble counter when she hit the floor and went straight to lullaby land. Then Tamara gave the other sister a grim look and went after her. But, after seeing what she did to her oldest sister, she let Sparkle go. She shook her head, threw her hands in the air and said: "Fuck This Shit!"

Well, it was long and painful ride home. Their wounded bodies would need nursing for the next 48 hours, at least. But, during the ride back home, the prevailing thought on their minds was that they paid a hell of a price for two hundred dollars and a second-place trophy, but it was worth it.

CHAPTER EIGHTEEN
LAVADA'S LAMENTATION

As they rode back from across-town the sun was coming up. The night of Hip-Hop- fever was over; however, a morning of unsettling drama was ahead.

Earlene had been on her usual route to the bathroom several times before Tamara and the other girls came home. But every time she tried to use the third-floor bathroom someone was always in it. So, she had to resort to using the bathroom downstairs on the first floor. Well, this seemed odd to her because someone was still using it when she returned to use it again later that morning.

Anyway, this time she walked closer to the door to knock on it and heard the sound of someone moaning like they were in pain. So, she knocked again to find out who it was, and the response she heard was "Go Away! Leave me alone!" And as of that moment, Earlene knew who it was and that something was wrong.

It was apparent from the sound of her moaning and groaning that something was seriously wrong. So, the first person she told was Tamara, who was just about to get in the bed. But, despite the roller-rink-rumble she had just been through, she reluctantly obliged her sister's request and went to see what was going on.

Well, it was logical reasoning that pointed to the fact that it had to be Lavada locked in the bathroom, because all the other girls were present and accounted for in the bed or somewhere around the house. When Tamara got to the bathroom, she asked if she was alright, and if she could do anything to help, but again, rather than divulging the truth, she shouted for them to go away.

And as such, Tamara sensed the stress in her voice and knew that something wasn't right. She turned to Earlene and whispered: "go get Lee," while she stayed by the door talking to her and reassuring her that whatever she was going through, everything was going to be alright.

In a matter of minutes, Earlene returned with Lee. He was worried and anxious when he heard that something was wrong with Lavada, and he tried to talk her into unlocking the bathroom door. And, he got so far as calming her down to the point where she attempted to get up to unlock the bathroom door, but as she got up from the toilet, they heard her fall. She had lost so much blood that it weakened her, and immediately after hearing her fall, he busted the door open and rushed inside.

It was worse than they could imagine—blood was all over the place—on the toilet seat, on the floor, and still oozing from her private area. Lee sat her up against the wall and held her in his arms; Earlene ran to get some towels from the linen closet down the hall and Tamara walked over to the toilet and looked inside--barely able to stomach the sight.

The sight of it gagged her. She immediately covered her mouth with her hand to keep from throwing up, but at the same time, after recognizing that there was a partially developed fetus sitting in a pool of blood in the toilet, she threw up anyway and flushed the toilet.

And as such, Tamara's heart went out to Lavada. She stood there with a bewildered look on her face; thinking to herself that this little girl must have been going through Hell. She had been up all night long having a miscarriage--suffering by herself because she didn't trust anybody enough to confide in them about her problem. No-one had a clue as to what was going on with her. Anyway, Tamara kept silent about Lavada's problem. The only person who needed to know the truth about this situation at that time was Grandma.

And, by the time Earlene returned with the towels and washcloths from the linen closet, she noticed the troubled look in Tamara's eyes. From the look in her eyes, Earlene knew that something unspeakable had happened. She asked Tamara if she was alright, but there was no response; just a long gazing stare and complete silence. But, when she finally responded, she abruptly told Earlene: "We need an ambulance quick! I'm going to talk to Grandma."

Tamara kept Lavada's miscarriage to herself. She was told her Grandmother about it, but she was afraid about how Lee would respond it he found out what had happened-- there was no telling how he would react. And if Earlene knew the truth right now, she would run the risk of her telling everybody in the house, so she just kept that news between herself and her Grandmother.

Anyway, soon after Tamara confided in her Grandma, she immediately called the 911 emergency operator. Fifteen minutes later, they were riding in the back of the ambulance with Lavada on their way to the hospital.

Over the next few days, no-one was the wiser or closer to the truth about Lavada's problem. They all went to visit her in the hospital, but the story behind her being in there was kept plain and simple—she was having severe cramps because of complications with her menstrual cycle. This tale set well for everyone but her brother Lee; he knew it was much more to it than that, but seeing how his Aunt Ella and Tamara were doing so much to cover up the real details, he decided to go along with them for the time being.

So, as it turned out, during those next few days, Lavada finally confided in Miss Ella and Tamara about the secret that she had been afraid to tell anyone. And as such, she explained to them that her stepfather had been sexually abusing her. And that he threatened to harm her mother if she told her brother, and that he threatened to harm her brother if she told her mother. Either way, this young thirteen-year-old girl was scared to death, and she saw no other course of action but to do what her stepfather told her to do. Therefore, after Miss Ella heard her story, she was outraged, but she knew just what to do.

There was no doubt that if Lee had found out what their stepfather had been doing to his sister he would have tried to kill him, and he would've wound up in jail for the better part of his life. Instead of letting that happen, Miss Ella used her influence to save Lee from himself, and at to put their bastard of a stepdad behind bars. She called her friend, who was a councilwoman at city hall. And, after they discussed the issues about what he did to her great-niece, a warrant for their stepfather's arrest was issued-- the police locked him up that very same day.

CHAPTER NINETEEN

THE ROPE A DOPE

Friday, August 12th. Leon and Leroy were in a funky mood. They wanted to do something-- anything to get out of the funky mood they were in. Leon's weed supply was gone, and his signs of signs of weed withdrawal were showing. His exuberant laughter was a spiritless solace of silence.

A more practical problem was nagging Leroy. He was worried about replacing the amount of money he spent out of his drug sales. He needed to make a quick hustle to make up money that wasn't really his to spent; he was mad at himself, and also disgusted with his surroundings. Being in that part of town affected his regular source of cash flow, and the exasperation of it all had reached its peak. It showed in his fidgety actions and reactions he had toward anyone that came around him.

And as such, with their situation being the way it was, later that morning, they broke camp and went on a mission to do something about it.

Leroy's desperate attitude led him to the thought of just pistol whipping one of the local dope boys in the neighborhood and robbing him. But, surprisingly, Leon definitely didn't want to be involved in anything like that, and he had the clarity to talk him about an idea that wouldn't lead to a lifetime of repercussions. Case in point, his Grandfather being on the run all the time because someone was always hot on his ass.

So, they both decided that if they were going to do anything illegal it would be a quick Sting that they couldn't be held accountable for anything that went down.

Anyway, the area where they planned to pull off their thoughtfully devised plan was about a half mile from Miss Ella's house. And although they were in the same rundown neighborhood, it was further up the road.

This area was more populated. There were businesses on one side of the street, with a pony-keg, a liquor store, a pawn shop, and grocery store. Furthermore, there were some old-rundown houses and apartment buildings sitting in the back of an alley. On the other side of the street there was a high school for performing arts, and a baseball field that stretched from one end of the block to the other. Therefore, the activity in that area included summer school kids going back and forth from one side of the street to the other, with a constant flow of bicycle cops from an inner-city precinct that frequently patrolled the area.

Leroy and Leon had a dangerous mission in mind. Yet and still, they combined their street savvy, took note of the area, and observed the activities and elements in the surrounding them and put all the pieces together in a plausible plan. They came up with one idea after another at first, and nothing seemed to work. But finally, they came up with a plan that they could both agree on and that they were 99% sure would work. But it was going to take the help of one more player and that player was Lee; whom they were pretty sure they could talk into helping them.

But they knew that imploring his help would come at a nominal price, and that price happened to be a bucket of chicken and a two liter of coke. Anyway, their next order of business was talking to some of the scumbags in the area to see who would lead them to the drugs. Being new faces in that part of town also meant that there would be trust issues, so keeping a low profile was utmost and necessary to keep from scaring away any prospective leads. Nonetheless, it took some time, but they eventually stumbled onto an O.G. who was a skeptic at first, but he was reluctantly willing to accommodate their needs.

Earlier that morning, they had put the word out on the streets that they were looking for a half pound of cocaine and a pound of some gangster weed. However, in reality all they had enough money for was an Eight-Ball and a Quarter-pound of weed. Anyway, that exchange of information was enough to lead them to the only person that could supply that kind of demand. He was a tall, black dread-lock from Jamaica who lived in the West-End-- Jamaican Joe.

As it turned out, Leroy knew him because he use to hang out in his neighborhood at times, but he didn't know Leroy in the least. Nevertheless, true to the game, Leroy still mustered up enough nerve to approach the scary looking dread to make his bid for some product.

Joe had just sat down inside a black Ford Escalade at the corner of the busy intersection. So, he walked to the passenger side window and tapped on it. Then he signaled him to roll his window down.

Leroy said: "Hey O.G. I need to holler at you, man." Joe said: "Get inside." Leroy got in the car and immediately said: " Hey my man, I need an eight-ball and a quarter pound of bud." Jamaican Joe said: "What makes you think I can get those things for you, little nigga, I don't know you!" Leroy said: "Ah, come on O.G. I know you roll in the best circles, and you hang with some of my people from out the way.

"I know you know one-eye Johnny and Bobby Williams O.G." And sure enough, when he heard those names, he just chuckled to himself and said: "Yeah I know, Eyeball." Then Leroy mentioned Bobby Williams and got an even more favorable reaction from him. Then Joe asked Leroy: " Is Bobby still fighting those Pitt-bulls?" Leroy said: "Yeah man, Bobby loves those Pitt-bulls, ain't no way he's going to stop fighting them, at least until they're all dead."

Well, fortunately for Leroy, knowing who he knew went a long way. Jamaican Joe turned to look Leroy in his eyes and asked him: "What do you go by." Leroy sat back looking puzzled by the question; not knowing how to answer. Then he asked him: "Your name, what's your name, little brother?" But, hesitantly, not wanting to reveal his real name, Leroy quickly made up a name before he answered and told him: "Skycap, they call me Skycap." Joe said: "Skycap! Why is that?" Leroy said: "Because I'm going make so much goddamn money one day, it's going to reach the sky."

Jamaican Joe just chuckled and said: "Look here Sky-crap, don't waste my fucking time. Do you have money?" Leroy slowly reached in his back pocket and pulled out a thick roll of money with hundred-dollar bills wrapped on the top and started peeling them back one at a time. He said: "Oh yeah, I got the money O.G." "O.G. looked at the money and said: "That's what I'm talking about-- one hour. Be here in front of this store in one hour and someone will meet you with your package, Solid." "Solid." "One more thing, don't try to FUCK ME! -----I GOT A GRAVEYARD MIND, A TOMBSTONE DISPOSITION, AND I DON'T MIND DYING!

Well, Leroy got out of the car feeling a little bit shaken by what he said, but he was also thinking that phase one of their plan was in effect, and regardless of what he said, Leroy had already accepted the fact that it was either (get rich or die trying when it came to hustling in the street). Anyway, he got his mind back on the most important part of the plan, and that was having Lee ride Earlene's bicycle to the store dressed like a Cincinnati Bicycle cop. From that point on, Leroy could implement a Sting that would wind up in a chase scenario. They knew it would take some convincing on Lee's part to get Earlene's bicycle from her, but if anybody could do it, he would be the one. They figured that if he told her that he was picking up something for, Lavada that she would do it, especially after her recent ordeal.

And, although it was almost a sure thing that they could tempt Lee with a bucket of chicken and a two liter of Coke, he still had to dress right for the part. It was important for him to wear short pants and head-gear. That way he would look like a cop by wearing the same kind of clothes and head-gear the cops wore.

Well, now it was just a matter of time before they could start phase two of operation "Rope-a-Dope."

And as such, the proxy that Jamaican Joe sent to deliver the package was his younger brother, AKA ----Raw-Dawg. He was standing in front of the store inconspicuously looking around to see if he could find someone who fit the description of the contact he was supposed to meet. When Leroy saw Raw-Dawg, he approached him and whispered a few words to him to let him know that he was the mark; after that, he introduced him to Leon. He told him that Leon was going to be their look-out man from the street while they took care of business.

So, with that information being known, Leroy and Raw Dawg walked through the recesses of a long alley and went inside a condemned building at the other end.

After that, Leroy did his best to stall for enough time for Lee to pedal up on Earlene's bicycle to meet Leon. And while they were inside the building, Leroy took his time inspecting the size, weight, smell, and the taste of the product.

Well, they hadn't been inside that abandoned building for more than five minutes and Leroy had to wonder if he'd have enough time for the final phase of the operation to work.

But luckily, the timing was just right, Lee showed up wearing a blue cotton shirt, Bermuda shorts, sneakers, and a safety helmet that made him look just like a bicycle cop, and likewise, Leon played his role as the lookout man. He stopped Lee on the street at the end of the alley and hollered "5-0 coming, 5-0 coming!"

When Leroy heard him shouting, and he cautiously cracked open the door to look. And damned if he didn't nearly go into panic mode himself when he saw Lee sitting on the bike looking identical to a CPD Cop. Furthermore, Lee unknowingly authenticated his presence as a cop by shouting down the alley at Leroy: "Hey, what you doing down there?"

Hearing Lee's deep voice was enough for Raw Dawg to panic. He gave Leroy a scouring look and shouted: "You set me up Goddammit," then he stuck his package down the front of his pants and jetted out the door.

And, just like that, Raw Dawg was completely unaware that he was doing exactly what Leroy and Leon wanted him to do. Because, when Lee rode down the alley towards the building to meet up with Leroy, he saw him dart out the building running top speed right behind Raw Dawg. Lee had no idea why Leroy was running, but he knew that he wasn't about to let Leroy slip out on the deal for that bucket of fried chicken. So he chased after Leroy while he followed Raw-Dog down the alley to a side-street, and watched him haul ass.

Well, even though Leroy was several yards behind, he was still hot on his tail and he never took his eyes off of Leroy. And as such, the realism of being a cop in pursuit of a suspect that Lee unknowingly caused by pursuing, Leroy produced the genuine effect of fear in Raw Dawg. And, with two strike on his record, getting a third strike by being caught by the police was on Raw--Dawg's mind.

Anyway, the continuous pursuit from this sequence of actions forced an even more significant reaction. Raw--Dawg kept looking back and saw what he thought was a cop right behind Leroy and he panicked. He knew for sure that they would get caught. So, he started unloading everything he had on him—his gun, his knives, and for sure, the drug packages he had on him. He threw everything in a trash dumpster around the next corner and kept on running.

By the time Leroy reached the next corner, he heard the sound of the dumpster lid shut, and he saw just enough of Raw Dawg's ass running up the street to let him know that they had hit a grand slam.

When Lee caught up with him, he saw Leroy reach inside the dumpster and take something out—he quickly stuck it down the crotch of his pants. But, before he could figure out what was going on, Leon had caught up with them, and he was ecstatic, and the jubilation in his silly sounding laugh was back.

After that, everything was everything. Leroy bought Lee that bucket of chicken, and a six-pack of coke. He gave Leon a heaping-helping of weed to keep him happy, and they brought Lavada a big, stuffed teddy-bear and some chocolate candy. And as such, Leroy was 'Back on the Block'.

CHAPTER TWENTY

THE FREE-STYLE FREE FALL

It was Saturday, August 13th, the day of the Cincinnati Free-Style Rap Festival. Aspiring rappers and several famous performers were expected to be here. Washington Park was the spot, and the first prize was a thousand dollars and a recording contract with a major recording studio.

Ernie and Monty were entered in the competition. They were confident in their ability as rappers and they were hoping that this would be their short ladder to stardom. They had been practicing their rap style from the first day they got to their Grandma Ella' house. Every spare minute they had was spent on rhyming lyrics and synchronizing them to different rhythms and beats.

However, they weren't the only aspiring rappers in the house. Earlene and Angie had signed up for the competition, and they had been spending a lot of time practicing their unique style of rap too. So, as it turned out, this event was an opportunity for all of them to compete. There was a diverse group of talented rappers entered in the competition and to earn some sort of recognition as legitimate rap artist here meant a lot to them.

Ernie and Monty were signed up under the stage name 'The Master Blasters. Earlene and Angie were signed up under the stage name 'The Elements of Surprise.' And despite the hot, early morning heat and humidity, hundreds of people were showing up; piling into the park while the final assembly of the stage was still in progress.

It was 12:00 pm, and the show was scheduled to start at 1:00 pm. And as the time lingered by, feelings of nervousness took its toll on them. Ernie and Monty were no exception; they knew that this was shake and bake time. They also knew that having a good performance was going to depend on them being clear and concise with the delivery of their rap and a confident stage presence.

On the same note, this was Earlene and Angie's first time in front of a large crowd as well; however, they were sure that the content of their rap lyrics and their lewd, lascivious sexual stage performance would win the appeal of the crowd. They were going to do whatever they had to do to win that thousand-dollar first place prize.

Meanwhile, back at Grandma Ella's house, it was impossible to know where every member in her house was throughout the day, but she surely knew the whereabouts of the four rap star wanna-ta- bees. And although she was reluctant about them going to this event--because of the violence she thought would break out, she gave in to their plea to go after she found out they had already paid their contest admission fees.

Furthermore, it turned out that Miss Ella's other brother, Lester was in town. He and his girlfriend had driven down from Detroit the other night; however, she had no idea that he would be dropping by her house unexpectedly. In addition to that, her daughter, Erma-Jean was back in town. She had found an apartment and had finally gotten settled in. She also planned a surprise trip to her mama's house to take Earlene and Tamara back home with her.

Anyway, back at the festival, it was do or die time. The judges had barely made it through the top of the list of rappers, and everyone that got on stage so far had been heckled and booed of the stage. And a s the contest continued, new rappers found out what they were made of, and some of them found out that their aspiring rap careers were now a thing of the past.

Nevertheless, Ernie and Monty were the next rappers on deck. They were finally going to get their chance to shine, and as nervous as they were, they still got on that stage and gave it all they had.

Ernie's spit:

I live in the suburbs—I go to private school—I learn my nouns and verbs, just like I should. But when I start to talking to my brothers in the Hood--I sound like a nerd when I'm thinking that I'm good—And when I get home—shit ain't much better—got to live like a saint—and ain't got a damn bit of cheddar.

Monty's spit:

I live downtown, around a bunch of clowns. I reside in the city--and it's a goddamn pity.

Niggas talk shit, and lurk in the alley, sucking on a dick just to make a tally. Expletives and adjectives are all I ever hear—said in strife to describe a way of life—hood-rats here, crackheads there-- in the goddamn alley--even sleeping on the stairs.

Together spit:

Uptown downtown, where ever we go—got to get my shit together—make a cash-money

Roll. Uptown downtown, wherever we go—gonna get our shit together—make that cash

Money flow.

Uptown downtown, where ever we go—got to get my shit together—make a cash-money

Roll. Uptown downtown, wherever we go—gonna get our shit together—make that cash

Money flow.

Ernie's spit:

Frowns all around me—over here, over there—coming from the honkies—all they do is stare.

Don't want no pity—ain't got no shame—all I want to do is play that cash money game.

Monty's spit:

Rats and roaches run through the halls. Shit on the stairs—piss on the walls.

If I open up a book—niggas think I'm a fool. And ain't a damn thang cool when you living around some ghouls. Teachers don't care—ain't a damn thing fair—got to wear a damn gas mask just to breath the fuckin air.

Together spit:

Uptown downtown, where ever we go—got to get my shit together—make a cash-money

Roll. Uptown downtown, wherever we go—gonna get our shit together—make that cash

Money flow.

Uptown downtown, where ever we go—got to get my shit together—make a cash-money

Roll. Uptown downtown, wherever we go—gonna get our shit together—make that cash

Money flow.

Ernie and Monty 'rocked the house,' the crowd cheered, applauded their showmanship. and gave them a standing ovation. Furthermore, to add to their successful performance, they got a spot in the super showdown to compete with the ten-best semi-finalist.

Earlene and Angie were so excited and proud of their performance that they exercised their exclusive rights to hug their cousins and showered them with kisses as soon as they got off the stage. And, needless to say, the needle on their cockiness meters sprang up to full. and their heads swelled to the size of melons. Earlene and Angie were inspired by their performance, and it gave them the determination to do just as good or better with their performance.

Back at the house, Lester and his girlfriend had pulled up through the back alley. He was driving a bran new black Cadillac with gold, spoke hubcaps. He parked across the alley and him and his girlfriend got out and made their way to the back gate where they saw Samantha sitting next to Rah-Mel's cage. Lester spoke to her and said: "Hey, baby girl, what's your name? She said "Samantha" and Samantha asked: "Who are you?" "I'm Lester, baby doll, and this is Miss Dorthy. But, from his cage, Rah-Mel growled at them--and Samantha quickly told him to hush.

Anyway, Lester didn't have time to pay attention to Rah-Mel's growling, his sense of smell picked up on the aroma of collard greens cooking through the screen door, so he went up the steps to the backdoor and knocked on it and hollered inside: "Hey, anybody home." Nobody answered, so he knocked and hollered again: "Hey, Sis—you in there?"

Well, a part of Miss Ella's weekend routine was watching Saturday afternoon wrestling. She and the girls were sitting in the front room with their eyes and attention glued to the television. They were watching the wrestling match of the century—laughing at Hulk Hogan and Andre the Giant in a super showdown match. It was something about watching these two big men go at it in the ring, and hearing them talk smack that just tickled her to pieces.

Anyway, after his knocks and hollers went unanswered, Lester decided to come inside and make himself at home. He grabbed a bowl and a fork and dug into that pot of collard greens and cornbread sitting on the stove. Well, it just so happened that at the same time he was digging in to Miss Ella's collard greens, she was taking a break from the TV to go check on them, and when she saw a stranger sitting at her table with his head buried in a bowl wolfing down her greens she was irate.

She immediately responded: "Nigga, what in the hell are you doing eating my greens?" Lester just looked up at her with a broad smile on his face and showed her the empty bowl and said: "What greens?" She screamed: Lester! You Rascal, I should have known it was you. Boy how-- where did you come from. How long have you been here?" Lester got up and gave her a hug and introduced his girlfriend and told her that they had been in town since last night. Then he asked her: "How in the hell have you been, sis? She said: "I've been like I've always been—fine as a can of snuff and half as dusty."

Well, a few minutes following that loving moment, Erma Jean showed up. She stepped through the back door and immediately recognized her Uncle Lester standing next to her mother. She was ecstatic, and she shouted: "Hey, Uncle Lester!" then she ran over to him and hugged him. It had been more than twenty years since they saw each other. And when he saw how his baby niece had filled out, and that she was a full-grown woman with all her curves in the right places, he stood back and took a good gander at her body and shouted 'Ah……. -Sol-lossy'. But, after he expressed his appreciation for what he saw in front of him-- something that his jealous girlfriend would've been better off not hearing; soon afterwards, she turned into a 'Green-Eyed-Monster.'

Anyway, back at the festival, A.J. showed up with Leroy and Leon. Leroy was on a mission. He wanted to make some fast money and this was the perfect place to do it, but he needed A.J. to lead him to the people that liked to get high. And that being the case, they rambled through the park from one location to another, making stops along the way to sell and collect money for services rendered. However, Leroy wasn't the only one on a quest to corner the drug market. They ran across several Jamaican Dreads with the same intention in mind, and they were peddling the same two-toke action ganja that Leroy had auspiciously acquired,

Nonetheless, it was just a matter of time before the Tot-Lot-Posse showed up. They were a well-organized and disciplined platoon of twenty-five-foot soldiers, and they were stylish and intimidating when they entered the park. This militant squad of rebels walked into the park in double files of twelve men, with their leader, Black Ice at the helm. They were bare chested and wore, sleeveless blue jean jackets and faded jeans; with black arm bands, and a red, black, and green bandanna wrapped around their forehead. And from the look of things, some serious shit was about to jump off.

Although the park was considered neutral ground for both gangs, the posse had always laid claim to the ownership of it because it was in a part of city where they lived long before the Dreads had even moved to the West End. Furthermore, there was a lot of resentment because it was a well-known fact that the Tot-Lot-Posse's drug sales were on the decline because of the Jamaicans move to Cincinnati, and, Black Ice was determined to put a stop to it even if it meant taking out their leader, Jamaican Joe.

But, on another note, there were a lot of amusing situations occurring in the heart of the park. The rapping didn't cease to exist, on nor off the stage. Earlene had ran into a love interest and Angie was trying to run away from one. She was being stalked by a boy in the crowd that she didn't know and didn't want to know. There were several occasions when she had to tell him to 'Fuck Off' and to leave her alone, but the hard headed smart ass just kept on aggravating her.

And whether Earlene knew it or not; she was playing with fire. She had stars in her eyes when a good-looking dude at the festival started romancing her. And although he was a lot older than her, and she knew it, it didn't matter to her one bit. And before you know it, she was sitting on his lap kissing him and swapping slob; and at the same time, listening to his line of bullshit. She was so smitten by his charm that no-one could tell her that he wasn't 'Mr. Wonderful.'

Likewise, Monty was awestruck by a fabulous looking girl at the festival. She had teasingly lured him into her presence with her big, beautiful bedroom eyes and her seductive smile; she had his heart pounding like a drum and his hormones were howling like a hound-dog's barking. But his sudden infatuation didn't last for long. In the midst of him trying to get his Mack on, he was nearly 'Jacked' when her six-foot-three-inch muscle-bound boyfriend suddenly showed up and put his arm around her. Then they walked away hand in hand right in front of him, but not before he stared Monty down with his ass-kicking disposition.

Just the same, Ernie went through a similar situation when he was getting his Mack on with one of the finest girls he had ever seen. They were in a deep groove when Peaches showed up to blow his game. When she saw them together, she confronted him with the biggest lie she could come up with. That jealous, church crusading hypocrite told him that she was pregnant and that he was the baby's daddy right in front of the girl. Ernie was dumfounded--he didn't know what to say, and it knocked him right out the box when it came to having a chance with the girl. Peaches killed that romance before it could even incubate, and as such, Monty was outraged. He wanted to grab Peaches by her throat and choke the shit out of her. Instead, he stood and watched her proudly sashay away. He said to himself, "That's alright, What Goes Around Comes Around, You Rotten Bitch!"

Nevertheless, back at Miss Ella's house, after an hour or so of mingling with the girls and reminiscing with his big sister, the spiteful eyes of Lester's girlfriend continued to follow and focus on both him and Erma Jean. But Erma Jean continued to go out of her way to be friends with the lady. She tried to get along with her and tried to get to know the things she liked to do. But, for some reason, girlfriend's mind was set on thinking the worse. She knew that Lester was a lady's man, and a well-seasoned player. So, she was persistent with her funky, disdainful attitude towards them.

In despite of that, Erma Jean still played it cool. She remained calm and collected regarding the lady's suspicious nature and her unusual circumstance. But, the snide comments and snobbish remarks that she didn't think Erma Jean heard behind her back were definitely taking a toll on her patience.

Anyway, the fun and laughter continued, and so did his girlfriend's funky behavior. Lester wasn't paying her any attention at all, and that in itself pissed her off. Besides that, the conversations he had were exclusively with the members of the family. However, it just so happened that his girlfriend overheard him and Erma Jean talking about going to the rap festival in town together and it set her on fire.

Anyway, Lester's attention was abruptly sidetracked by the car pulling in the driveway--it was Riley and Alvin. And during same moment that, Lester stepped off the porch to start walking towards the car, his girlfriend turned to Erma Jean and spewed her venom: "I'll be damned if you go anywhere with my man, Tramp." And accordingly, Erma Jean's fuse was lit. She looked at her with fire in her eyes and said "Bitch! I know you didn't call me a tramp!" Then the woman rolled her eyes at her and drew back like she was going to smack, Erma Jean. But in the split second that followed, all that was heard was a loud crack and a thump; Erma Jean jacked her jaw, and she was laying in the yard flat on her back. But, Erma Jean wasn't through with her ass yet.

Because before Lester even reached the car, he heard Alvin yelling at him, and pointing to what was going on behind him. And, when he turned around and looked, he saw Erma Jean straddled over his girlfriend with a brick in her hands--ready to split her wig. And without giving the situation a second thought, he ran back to the yard and grabbed his girlfriend by her feet and drug her little ass through Erma Jean's legs, just as she was coming down with that brick to scramble her brains.

Well, after that, Lester couldn't rightly blame Erma Jean for what she did; he knew that sooner or later his girlfriend's big ass mouth was going to write a check that her little ass couldn't cash. So, he picked her up and carried her in the house and revived her. And, when she came to, and realized what happened, she couldn't wait to call a cab and get as far the fuck away from that house as fast as she could. And as such, being fed up with his girlfriend and all of her shit, his flat-out sentiment was good-bye and Good Riddance!

Meanwhile, back at the festival, it was approaching 3:00 pm; Washington Park was packed with shoulder-to-shoulder rap lovers. The many vendors from the city were there selling hotdogs, pop, potato chips and all the usual amenities that a festival provided. Lester and Erma Jean had just made it there. They parked a half mile away and had to walk the distance due to the lack of parking spaces. And once inside, they had to wiggle and squirm their way through the crowd to find a good seat to view the stage. Nonetheless, they had arrived right time because Earlene and Angie had just been called up to the stage to give their performance.

And damned if they weren't true to their stage name "The Elements of Surprise," because their stage performance was synonymous to what happened next. Erma Jean, Lester, and the crowd were sure as hell surprised. These girls got on stage and spit out some of the lewdest lyrics imaginable. Furthermore, they were dressed like two Bengal tigers, wearing orange and black striped spandex body suits, fur boots, and cat-like designer sunglasses.

Earlene's spit:

Hey little mama's boy, what cha gonna do, I've been saving this good stuff especially for you.

You say you wanna Hit It, so come on now and get it. I ain't got no time to play, so you better come today. Hey, little mama's boy, if you're really hung, come and get this good stuff, come and get you some. I need me a real man to make my Kitty Cum.

Angie's spit:

Hey little mama's boy, what cha gonna do, I got some chocolate pudding here for you, and Umm it's yummy too. Now if you can't handle it, or if you're afraid, I'll find me a real man to hit it all day. And if you need a Hoochie, with some real good Coochie--I am the one for you, come and make my Kitty Cum.

Together spit:

Scratch my Kitty Cat, and Lick my Clit—I need me a real man to take away my Itch.

Scratch my Kitty Cat, and Suck my Tits—I need me a real man—a man who won't Quit.

Scratch my Kitty Cat, and Lick my Clit—I need me a real man to take away my Itch.

Scratch my Kitty Cat, and Suck my Tits—I need me a real man—a man who won't Quit.

Scratch my Kitty Cat, and Lick my Clit—I need me a real man to take away my Itch.

Scratch my Kitty Cat, and Suck my Tits—I need me a real man—a man who won't Quit.

Scratch my Kitty Cat, and Lick my Clit—I need me a real man to take away my Itch.

Scratch my Kitty Cat, and Suck my Tits—I need me a real man—a man who won't Quit.

Those girls enticed very male hormone in the vicinity of the stage and then some; however, they didn't get to finish their performance. It took a while, but Erma Jean recognized the voices on stage and she put two and two together, and when she came up with the correct analysis she told her Uncle Lester: "That's Earlene and Angie on that Goddamn Stage!" And just like 'A Mad Black Mother', she squirmed her way from the middle of that crowd all the way to the front of that stage and shouted: "Bitch are you Crazy! Get your Ass off that Stage!"

Earlene was in shock and she was embarrassed. The embarrassment was written all over her and Angie's faces. And to add to the dismay, the male members in the crowd were so disappointed when she made them leave the stage that they started booing and shouting obscene language at Erma Jean; she pulled the plug on the show, but she was determined to hold steadfast to what she was doing--she cursed right back at them. It was blessing that her Uncle Lester was there; he had her back all the time. However, after he saw that the girls were safely in her custody, and that she had safely secured them, someone in the crowed recognized him and shouted his name--they were some old friends of his and an old flame of his from the past, so he wondered off from Erma Jean and the girls for a while.

Nevertheless, and not surprisingly, the one person in the crowd that found pleasure during Earlene and Angie's stressful moment was, Peaches. She and some of her girlfriends were standing right beside the stage when Erma Jean abruptly abducted them. She was also close enough to exploit their situation with her vindictiveness. "Peaches shouted: "Who's the Ho now, Ho? Poor little pussycats. Mama's got to take you home and give you a bowl of milk to cool your hot asses off now-- don't she."

Well, as hard as it was for them to restrain themselves from retaliating, they did—anyway for the time being. However, the barrage of insults from Peaches and her entourage kept on coming. They were called them Ho's, sluts, tramps, and bitches all during Erma Jeans escorting them to her car—and, up until the time that Angie's obnoxious admirer grabbed her by the ass and disappeared in the crowd she would have been fine.

But, without a doubt, all hell broke loose after that. Angie was pissed about all that was going on at the moment, and the shit he did to her was just too much to let slide by without doing something about it. She immediately bolted like a wild colt and went on a search and destroy mission to find and confront that bastard. Therefore, right after Angie busted a move, Earlene bolted in the opposite direction; her adversary was in plain sight—a few feet away. Erma Jean couldn't do a damn thing about it except stand their looking confused. She was stuck having to make a split decision—which one to go after.

Anyway, after a short pondering of the thought, she decided to go after Angie because she was afraid that Angie might be in more danger than Earlene. Besides, she knew that Ernie and Monty were a few feet away, so she told them to keep an eye on Earlene--and make sure she doesn't kill anybody.

While on the warpath, Earlene pushed her way through a crowd of people to reach Peaches and her girlfriends, But she didn't say a word when she reached them, she just walked up to, Peaches and slapped her upside her head. The powerful sting from her slap was so devastating that it had Peaches seeing stars.

All Peaches could do was stagger backwards into the arms of her girlfriends; they had to help holding her up. And, with vengeance on her mind, Earlene wasn't through with the heifer yet. She hollered: "What you going to do now, Pretty Bitch!" Well, Peaches eventually regained her focus and ran toward Earlene swinging her arms--scratching and clawing at Earlene's face.

Well, Ernie and Monty were on the sidelines watching like spectators in an audience; they got a kick out of seeing Peaches get her ass kicked—especially Ernie, who felt like the bitch deserved to get her ass kicked for blowing his game earlier. Therefore, he wasn't going to do a damn thing to stop it. However, later on he changed he mind. He saw Earlene sitting on top of Peaches batting her head back and forth like it was in a pinball machine. Peaches was laying on the ground unconscious, and he remembered what his Auntie had said, so both him and Monty had to pull Earlene off of her.

Well anyway, getting back to the park, Leon, Leroy, and A.J. were still hanging tough. Leroy was making a killing selling his weed and his ready-rock to all the well-known pot-heads and crack heads that A.J. knew. However, on the flip side, it never occurred to them that A.J. was about to introduce them to Raw-Dawg. Raw-Dawg had a booth set up at the rear end of the park selling oils and incense, so as they casually walked up to his booth, Raw-Dawg and Leroy immediately locked eyes, and before A.J. could open his mouth to say a word, Raw-Dawg opened up his mouth and said: "I knew I'd see you Motherfuckers again," then he reached underneath his table for his nine and pointed it them. But, at the same, it was a standoff, because Leroy had pulled his 38 bulldogs from the back of his belt and had it pointing at Raw-Dawg.

Raw Dawg shouted: You got the money you owe me, Motherfucker?" Then Leroy shouted: "I don't owe you jack, Nigga!" A.J. said: "Money? What money? They my cousins, Dawg." Those two Motherfuckers set me up, they the Goddamn Police! Naw, Dawg—you wrong. I swear they my cousins, man." "All I know is that those two Motherfuckers Fucked me out of a quarter pound and an eight-ball. Now, either they the police or 'I'm Boo-Boo The Fuckin Fool!' Shit if Joe wasn't my brother he would've killed my as over that shit. As a matter of fact, I'm calling him right now."

Nonetheless, during the half-second that it took Raw-Dawg to look at the numbers on his phone to dial Jamaican Joe's number—Leon and Leroy split from the scene like a flash of lightning. A.J. stood there watching them run away with a puzzled look of innocence on his face. He just knew that it was All Over for their asses if they got caught, and he knew it was All Over for his ass if he didn't start kissing ass like a professional negotiator.

Nevertheless, backtracking to, Erma Jean. She had finally caught up with Angie, and she saw that she Angie had finally caught up the ugly son-of-a-bitch that grabbed her ass. He was in a crowd with his other Dread-Lock friends; surrounded by a cloud of ganja smoke. However, Erma Jean watched from close by while that petite, fearless little girl walked straight up to that boy and slapped the shit out of him. And naturally, his buddies were shocked when they that unbelievable assault on his manhood--although it didn't stop them from laughing at his stupid ass. But, seconds after the shock from that slap wore off, out of humiliation, that boy turned around with a backhand slapped Angie to the side of her face; it was so hard that it knocked her on her ass.

Well, when Erma Jean saw him slap her, she didn't hesitate to bust a move. She walked straight up to that boy, looked him in the eye, and before he could blink, she punched him dead in his face with an overhand right. She deflated his ass like a busted balloon, and he hit the ground face first--that's when his boys stopped laughing—they didn't like seeing that shit. So, they slowly circled around her and Angie and started harassing both of them.

Well, from not too a far away, Uncle Lester got wind of what was going on and went to investigate. When he reached them, he was right on time. He witnessed a first-hand account of that pack of rats bullying and taunting his baby niece. And as such, things went too far. One of the boys drew his fist back to hit Erma Jean in her face. But all of a sudden, and before anybody knew what was happening, Lester was right behind that asshole. He snatched the boy's arm with one hand, and in his other hand, he had his 38-caliber snub-nose pressed right upside that boy's head. He said: "Just Breath Motherfucker!

Just breath. Be thankful and thoughtful that I haven't blown your goddamn brains out yet, and that I still can."

He most assuredly he got the message, and so did the rest of his friends. After that, Erma Jean and Angie left with Lester and started on their way back to get Earlene. But the drama wasn't over yet, because all of a sudden, they heard the sound of semi-automatic gunfire ripple through the park. Then they heard someone shouting: "They shot Ziggy! They shot Ziggy!" And the natural reaction from the people in the park was to hit the ground; they were scurrying all over the place in a panic. They ran to the streets to look for cover behind trees, cars, park benches or whatever they could find to keep from being shot.

Things had turned out with the Tot-Lot-Posse being in a war with the West-End Dreads. The Dreads were selling drugs on Tot-Lot turf, and as a result, gang warfare was breaking out everywhere in the park. Moreover, Black Ice had ordered a hit on Jamaican Joe; whom they thought was in the park at the time. But, they mistakenly killed his twin brother, Ziggy, who looked, dressed and wore his dreads down to the middle of his back—just like Joe did.

Furthermore, the security guards and the few police that patrolled the park were helplessly out- numbered, and out-gunned by armed gang members from both gangs.

After Jamaican Joe got the word that his brother was dead he went ballistic; he declared open season on anybody wearing a red, black, and green bandana. And as such, he and over a dozen of his henchmen pulled up in a pickup truck and reeked havoc on the civilian population of the park. They shot and maimed dozens of people just from being suspected of being a member of the Tot-Lot gang. And apparently, Leroy and Leon were caught up in the crossfire in an effort to flee from the terror driven destruction.

The retrospective thought in Uncle Lester's mind was that he hadn't seen this type of warfare since he left the jungles of Vietnam in 1969. However, he still knew how to be a soldier. He guided his group of family member to safety. He had them stay low and move swiftly behind the trees around the perimeter of the park, and use any natural obstacle they could find to protect them from the gunfire.

But, after what seemed like hours of terror and turmoil, dozens of police officers showed up as well as a SWAT team to flush out any snipers that might be in the area. By that time they had finally reached a safe place to exit the park, and fortunately, no-one in the family was seriously hurt; however, as they were leaving the park, they turned to take a final look and saw Leroy with his arm draped around Leon's shoulder limping toward them. Somehow Leroy got shot and had a stray bullet in his ass.

Yet, and still, the sight of seeing the dead and maimed bodies on the ground surrounding them was unbearable. Paramedics and rescue teams rushed to the scene; they were everywhere carting people off by the dozens; dozens of ambulances hurried to take them to the hospital, and Leroy was carted off on a stretcher right along with them.

Anyway, up until this time no-one had seen or heard from A.J. since the start of the conflict. They knew he was there, but until now, they hadn't given him a second thought, or even took the time to ask about him. Well, their wondering ended real quick when they all headed across the street to go back to their cars. They heard a voice shout down them and say: "Hey Yall, is it over yet. Is it safe?" But, when they stopped to look behind them, they heard nothing. So, they turned around and started walking again. But, they heard the voice again, and this time they all looked up and saw A.J. perched on a tree branch high above them--he was up there scouting the whole area to see if there was any danger of coming down, So, the obvious question they asked him was: "A.J., what are you doing in that tree?" A.J. said: "Shit! Are you kidding? There've been Attempts On My Life!"

CHAPTER TWENTY-ONE

AUNT ELLA'S MESSAGE/ THE CONCLUSION

What started out as a promising event for aspiring rap artist soon turned into a senseless slaughter. The Free-Style festival turned into a Free Fall for a disaster. At least a dozen ambulances and trauma teams showed up to care for the wounded and save the lives of the near-death victims--over a half dozen news teams were there to record the unprecedented event.

More than a few misfortunes in life are brought on by the emotions of greed, jealousy, envy, and that all powerful desire for revenge. And as such, the choices we make under these conditions—good or bad, are what we live with. Thus, in essence this is called "Life."

Anyway, the pranks and antics that went on under Miss. Ella's roof this summer were harmless and innocent, for the most part; however, in a world with so much chaos, confusion, and controversy, under different circumstances they could lead to more severe consequences—which is the lesson that Miss. Ella was trying to facilitate. She knew that there is good and bad in all of us--she referred to these elements as "Seeds of Temptation." She knew that they grow stronger as we get older and that without proper guidance they could lead to perilous outcomes. She also believed that the best way to reroute temptation and strong desires for revenge was with the guidance that comes from having strong morals and a strong family value system.

Therefore, the basis of her motive to have them attend church services with her every Sunday was to make them aware of the profound challenges that chosen people in the bible faced so that they might be able to face any future problems they may have. Furthermore, this wise, elderly woman knew that most of these kids lives had been allocated by single parent households--living with Grandparents or other family members; being brought up in foster homes, or just living in overall dysfunctional settings. She felt the need and the obligation to help these children learn who they were and the type of family they come from.

LESSONS FROM THE BIBLE

The Lesson from (Jonah)

"In the story of Jonah and the whale there is a lesson to be learned. Instead of Jonah doing what the Lord asked him to do, he turned away from the lord. He was deemed to be a curse to the men on the ship he was on and tossed in the sea and swallowed by a whale. After three days of giving praises to the lord he was released from the belly of the whale. And, that's when he decided to go to the city of Nineveh as the Lord instructed him to do. It was known for its wickedness, and it was also the capital city of Israel's fiercest enemy.

However, after he delivered his message from the Lord, he was surprised to see that the whole city, and even the King listened to him preach his warnings about the city being destroyed if they didn't repent.

So, they repented to the lord's will and the Lord forgave them. But, Jonah got mad at God after that because he had spared the lives of Israel's enemy. And, when Jonah left the city he stopped to rest under a vine that God provided to shelter him from the hot sun."

"But the next day God provided a worm to destroy the vine to teach him a lesson. So Jonah complained to God again. But this time God scolded Jonah. He told him "Why are you are so worried about this vine that you didn't create, and why shouldn't I worry about the 120,000 lost people in Nineveh who don't know their right hand from their left hand."

"And as such, Jonah learned a valuable lesson about the Lord's mercy and forgiveness. He learned that it extends to all people who repent and believe in the Lord--even his enemy, and he also learned that he should be a shining light to the people that have gone astray."

(Samson & Delilah)

"The story of Samson and Delilah lets us know how deceitful some women can be, and how a man can fall in love with a beautiful woman without thinking about the things that are important, and the things he should be doing. Samson's calling from birth was to begin the deliverance of Israel from Philistine oppression. But his downfall with Delilah cost him his great physical strength, his physical sight, his freedom, his dignity, and eventually his life."

"Delilah wore Samson down until he divulged the secret of his strength. And after she learned it, she turned him over to his enemy. Part of his Nazirite vow at birth was that he never cut his hair. Well, when the Philistines caught him they severed the braids of his hair, and he was helpless. His enemy poked out his eyes and humiliated him in front of the crowds of people who came to see the once great Israelite warrior."

"After that, they enslaved him and put him to work grinding grain. But, over time, his hair grew back, and he got his strength back, but the Philistines didn't pay attention to that. And in spite of his failures and sins, Samson's heart turned to the Lord. He was humbled. And for the first time, he prayed to God—and God answered him."

"Then one day they paraded him into the temple to entertain the crowds. But Samson got so mad that he braced himself between the two main support pillars of the temple and pushed with all his might. The temple came down killing Samson and all of the people in it. And when Samson did that, he destroyed more of his enemy than he had ever killed in all the battles of his life."

"Although he was a failure at one time, he still accomplished the mission that God-assigned him to do. So, the lesson from this is that Samson is just like you and me when we give ourselves over to sin. When we are in a state of sin, we can easily be deceived because the truth becomes impossible to see. But, no matter how far you've fallen away from God, and no matter how big you've failed, it's never too late to humble yourself and return to God."

(The Story of Job)

"The story of "Job" will also teach you a lesson. And that lesson is to 'always to keep your faith in God, and worship him despite the hardships that are in your life.' Job, was a man who had everything you can imagine in his time, He had it all: A large family, wealth, and blessings of every kind imaginable.

During that time, Job may have been the richest man on the face of the earth. The Bible says that "He had seven sons and three daughters, and he owned seven thousand sheep, three thousand camels, five hundred yokes of oxen, and five hundred donkeys, and he had a large number of servants. He was the greatest man among all the people of the East."

"But the Lord took it all away from him; just to show the devil that he would remain a faithful servant regardless of any downfall or misery that he suffered through. So, after the devil saw that he couldn't shake Job's faith in God by taking away his riches, nor his family and friends, he gave up. And after that, God made Job even richer than he was before with twice as many sheep, oxen, camels, and donkeys as before. Plus servants, and a new family with seven sons and three daughters. And he lived to be 140 years old."

(The Story of Abraham)

"Now the next story that you should have learned about in Sunday school is about Abraham. Abraham was a man who played an important role in the history of Islam, Judaism, and Christianity. In Islam, he is seen as a holy prophet. Judaism considers him to be the 'father' of their religion, and in Christianity, Abraham's lineage is seen as producing the World's Savior, Jesus Christ."

"As told in the Bible, God promised Abraham that he would be the father of many nations. But, at that time, Abraham was 99 years old and his wife, who had no children, was 90. Nevertheless, Abraham trusted God and believed God could accomplish what he had promised."

"But, as time went on, Sarah, Abraham's wife, was still childless, so she told Abraham to sleep with her handmaid so that they could get a child from that union. So, a son was born from that union, and his name was Ishmael."

"However, this wasn't in God's plan. God's promise was for the offspring of Abraham and Sarah's union, and eventually Isaac was born. He was the son that came from the union of Abraham and Sarah, and it was through Isaac that the many nations would be blessed."

"But, God still had to test Abraham. So, God told Abraham to: "Take your son, your only son Isaac, whom you love, and go to the land of Moriah, and offer him there as a burnt offering--or in other words kill him. So, Abraham was heartbroken, but he still did what the Lord had ordered him to do,"

"However, God intervened and stopped Abraham from killing his son at the very last second. And instead, the Lord provided a sacrifice in the form of a ram that was caught in the nearby brush. And as such, Abraham's faith had been tested and proved, by his obedience to God."

"The lesson from the story of Abraham is an example of how you should have genuine faith in God. And our faith should result in us doing good things. The faith that you have inside you should result in an outward change of your behavior. If it's doesn't, then you may not be of genuine faith at all."

THE CONCLUSION

"You children need to know that you are the 5th generation of great-grandsons and grand-daughters of Bedford and Liza Le Grand. Bedford Le Grand was born in1805 in North Carolina, and he was a slave, and everyone of you is a descendant of an African slave, and everyone of you is the descendant of an African slave that came from a bloodline of African Kings, Queens, and Warriors."

"Your greatness stems from your bloodline, and the blood inside you holds the key to what you have yet to realize. Until you know who you are, you will never do the great things that you are capable of doing.

Walk tall and be proud of who you are. Learn how to love yourself and respect all people to the best of your ability. Until you really know how to love yourself, you will never know how to love anyone else."

"Children, try to lead peaceful, productive lives and always give God the praises that are due to him. The tricky part about life is that God gave all of us free will to choose the direction and the way that we want to live our lives. But it's up to you to be smart and choose wisely. Let your faith in God grow, and from this day forward your hard work and your faith in god will get you through the hard times when everything else fails."

Most of these kids took to heart the message that Miss. Ella was telling them. They understood the correlation with the Bible stories and the things that were happening in their lives. The recollection of those four particular stories added knowledge and wisdom to their everyday lives and they had a profound effect on them and their decision making as individuals. And as such, most of them took heed to what she said and tried to start living their lives from the positive perspective that she provided for them.

Unfortunately, a few of them didn't, and continued on a path of needless mishaps and mayhem. But, Miss Ella knew that, that would happen too.

And sadly, six weeks later Miss Ella passed away. She had died was no-doubt in Heaven wearing the wings of an angel. Therefore, one of the largest funerals in the city of Cincinnati was held to honor her passing. Her friends and her relatives in from the all over the country flew in to show their respect to the grieving family members, and to view her body at peace.

During the funeral, tears flowed from the eyes of the immediate family and sadness overwhelmed their hearts. Furthermore, there was a sea of grave and gloomy faces filling that small, over-capacity Holiness church on that hill. And as the immediate family sat down front at a loss for words--

bereaving with tears from dismay and sadness, sudden burst of out loud crying echoed throughout the church.

Yet and still, the preacher read her obituary aloud. It told a long story about her endless accomplishments and contributions as a humanitarian, housewife, and as a lifelong mother dedicated to her children and family.

THREE YEARS LATER

Although A.J. regularly attended church with his Grandmother, he was burnt out on going to church now-- especially after the death of his Grandmother. He also had doubts about the existence of God. But, somehow that all changed. One day he was in a tragic car accident that could have left him for dead. But, his near death experience caused him to make a reassessment of God. And as it turned out, he resumed his belief in the power of God.

And, amazingly, the spirit of the Lord must have touched Walter as well, because, Walter turned his life around also, and as such, both of them focused on their God-given talents. A.J. got his real estate license and started flipping houses a few years later. He got married to an extraordinary woman, and now they have three kids and they are doing very well.

When Walter went back to Atlanta, he became a member of a church, and he was blessed to start working as a salesman for a well-known car dealership. Now, at twenty-five years of age, he is the top salesman in his area and he expects to have his own car dealership very soon.

Leon and Leroy were birds of a feather that strayed in a different direction. The bullet that found its way to Leroy's behind hadn't taught him much about life, and it wasn't the last time he got shot. Anyway, as soon as they turned eighteen, both of them did a stretch of time in the state penitentiary. Leon did a year in the pen with two years parole on the shelf. Leroy did a mandatory five years for selling drugs and the possession of an illegal firearm. However, they're doing fine now.

Leon got his GED when he was in jail, and he went through a 12-step program and stopped his drug consumption with pot. When he got out, he enrolled at the University of Cincinnati and is taking courses in abnormal psychology to get his bachelor's degree. He is now working as a drug counselor at a rehab facility.

Leroy finally did an about face and turned his life over to the Lord too. He went to truck driving school and is working as an over-the-road truck driver making enough money to get his mind off the fast money he made in the streets.

D.A. and Lee both had the physical size and the natural talent to play on a professional sports team. However, Lee turned down several scholarships offers to play football. Instead, he finished high school and was offered a position as a manager at a fast-food restaurant. And right now, he is a regional manager over a chain of Wendy's in Southwestern Ohio.

D.A. got a scholarship to play basketball at Eastern Kentucky University. But, he was soon disappointed. He played two years and injured his ACL. And although he recovered, he still felt that he would never be the same player that he had been. Therefore, he sacrificed his love for a career playing basketball and settled for a degree in corrections and a minor in recreation. He works as a Park Ranger in peak seasons, and as an assistant high school basketball coach during basketball season.

Little Gary—AKA—Popsicle, continued to go down a path of adverse trials and tribulations; he didn't get his act together until sometime later. Nonetheless, he was fortunate to have gone to prison as soon as he turned eighteen; if not, he more than likely would have wound up dead.

Anyway, during his three year stretch at O.P., he eventually opened his eyes and saw the light. He got his high school equivalency, and if wasn't for his love for money, he would have never found his God-given talent. He gained an interest in accounting, and when he got out of prison he went through a two year training course in accounting and adapted to a natural affinity for doing tax returns. He eventually got his B.S. Degree and now he works as a freelance tax return specialist and business consultant.

Monty and Ernie continued to follow through with their ability as rap artist. They started their own rap group, and they had professional careers as "The Master Blasters" performing in concerts all around the United States. Nonetheless, after three years their group broke up. However, Monty still lives in L.A. and he works behind the scenes as a music producer with various rap artist. But, Ernie followed his lifelong interest in photography and somehow he flipped it into a career in Hollywood as a cinematographer.

When it came to the girls, they found the courage to be proud of who they are, the power to change the things that they could change, and the wisdom to know the things they couldn't change.

Danielle and Sparkle went after what they wanted to do in the entertainment field. Sparkle wanted to be an actor on stage or in the movies, and Danielle wanted to be a dancer. They both attended a school of performing arts, and they followed up by taking professional classes in choreography and acting. Danielle eventually moved to New York City where she has performed in several Broadway musicals. Sparkle moved to L.A. where she was discovered by talent scouts that set her up in roles as an actor in several drama scenes at Paramount Studios in Hollywood. Nonetheless, both of them have been waiting for a breakout performances on stage and screen.

Lavada, made things simple for herself despite all her hard work getting a degree. She went to college and studied child psychology and became a child care specialist. She now works with children with disabilities and has a titled position in social work for the Department of Job and Family services.

Earlene and Angie got scholarships to attend Howard University and studied law. They both passed the Bar Exam and are now practicing attorneys. Earlene's specialty is in criminal Law and she works as a defense attorney in the Washington D.C. Court system. Angie's specialty is corporate law and she works as a special advisor and liaison collaborator on classified business assignments at the White House.

Well, after that memorable summertime experience in 1993 at their Grandma's house, the eldest cousins—Kim and Tamara decided to go into the business of saving souls. A few years after the death of their Grandmother, they both received their Doctorate Degrees in Theology. Then they later served as pastors in the local churches. And as of now, their aspirations to serve as pastors in their own newly built churches are becoming a reality. Their mission statement is to "Change the World One Soul at a Time."

Last but not least is ten-year-old Samantha, whom is now eighteen. She turned out to be the most phenomenal cousin out of the group. At the age of sixteen she was accepted into Harvard Law School, and she has been consumed with a passion to serve the public in the political arena. However, her deepest passion lies in her undying aspiration to become the first African American Woman President of the United States.

AUTHOR BIO

His Freelance writing career started in 1997, with the publication of his first young adult novel, "The Snowman in the Backyard." Soon afterwards, he earned his Bachelor of Arts degree in Journalism and Mass Communication and pursued work as a Freelance Journalist. As a freelance Journalist he contributed news stories to the Cincinnati Herald, pertaining to celebrity, TV Host Montel William's new online TV show; recently appointed Queen City Foundation Interim Director, Torilyn O'Neal, and Hamilton County Sheriff, Simon Lease. His past endeavor has been contributing stories as a Freelance Journalist to the Global, online news network, Blasting News. He has crafted and published an abundance of news and opinion stories with five-star ratings on everything from Racism in Education in America to Cyber Warfare Attacks. His most recent accomplishment has been with the publication of his new novel, "The Seeds of Temptation."

www.ingramcontent.com/pod-product-compliance
Lightning Source LLC
LaVergne TN
LVHW061936070526
838199LV00060B/3848